Inklings

ON PHILOSOPHY AND WORLDVIEW

GUIDEBOOK

 Tyndale House Publishers
Carol Stream, Illinois

Visit Tyndale online at tyndale.com.

Visit the author's website at IntheTrueMyth.org.

TYNDALE and Tyndale's quill logo are registered trademarks of Tyndale House Publishers.

Inklings on Philosophy and Worldview Guidebook

First edition published in 2014 by WheatonPress.com. Fourth edition published in 2017 as *Inklings on Philosophy, Theology, and Worldview Student Workbook* by Wheaton Press under ISBN 9780692227213. Fifth edition by Tyndale House Publishers in 2020.

Designed by Jennifer Phelps

Edited by Jonathan Schindler

For information about special discounts for bulk purchases, please contact Tyndale House Publishers at csresponse@tyndale.com, or call 1-800-323-9400.

ISBN 978-1-4964-2892-9

Printed in the United States of America

26   25   24   23   22   21   20
7   6   5   4   3   2   1

TABLE OF CONTENTS

A Note for Leaders

This companion book to *Inklings on Philosophy and Worldview* is meant to be used as a guidebook, like an adventure guidebook, except for the heart, soul, and mind. I have led students on rock climbing, backpacking, mountain climbing, ice climbing, and sailing adventures in various parts of our world. When I get to a gorgeous granite cliff with the hope of taking an eager group of voyagers up and down the steep facade, I always bring a professional guidebook with me. I use it to navigate the terrain, find the right spots, learn about the safety concerns, and plot out a course for the day of adventure and exploration. I also train my students in how to use the guidebook so that if they come back, they can safely and strategically lead themselves and others through the climb.

This is the conceptual framework of this book. It is meant to be a tool to help young people (and their leaders) grow on this adventure of life. Leaders must model the adventure and eventually master the material. At first the people you lead will be using the book with you as you learn the material together. However, like a repeated adventure trip to the same mountain, after several visits, the terrain and skills become more familiar and personal. The same is true for anyone using these texts and tools. After enough use, the leaders and youth applying this material will be able to eventually use it in their own way and even extend it into new learning and growth. This book and the supplemental material available on the InTheTrueMyth.org website are designed to guide you to extend your learning and process the information in the *Inklings on Philosophy and Worldview* book in a deeper and more practical way. The best rock-climbing guidebooks help me get to the base of the rock cliffs. When I find the climb I want to do, I then put the book down, get on my safety gear, and put my hands and feet on the actual rock and start climbing. My hope is that this guidebook gets used in a similar way.

My favorite guidebooks are annotated, drawn in, dog eared, tattered, torn, and worn with coffee stains and dirt. Similarly, when used well, this book should guide you in experiencing, interacting with, participating in, and processing the information and concepts in the *Inklings* book and well beyond. Guidebooks for rock climbing are designed to be used at the cliffs, to actually rock climb, but it's hard to climb with a book in your hands. These books and even the information in them are tools and means to the end, not the end themselves. Philosophy needs to be more than just thinking; it needs to be doing! Paul writes to the church at Corinth, "While knowledge makes us feel important, it is love that strengthens the church. Anyone who claims to know all the answers doesn't really know very much. But the person who loves God is the one whom God recognizes" (1 Corinthians 8:1-3). Philosophy that is worth anything will be put to use in lives that actually live the concepts.

Training is essential. Paul refers to it often in his letters to the early churches. Training implies repeated hard work and perpetually pushing oneself to become more adept and stronger. Coaches are often essential to help us focus and persevere, but ultimately the responsibility rests on the player or the student. On my own educational and spiritual journey, and after thirty years of teaching, I have learned that good books, great authors, and strong primary texts speak for themselves. As teachers, parents, and mentors, we need to get young people to actually read and personally engage with primary texts and their messages. Of course, guided discussion and helpful insights enhance and often unlock treasure chests of meaning. Nevertheless, the best resources we have at our fingertips, like Scripture, bear much more fruit the more we read them, the more we contemplate them, and the more we practice them. Furthermore, it is vital to read the Word of God in the context of the other primary sources offered in this text. This is one of the reasons why the publisher has put many of the Scripture readings right into this guidebook. This can help young people to see that Scripture is also a primary text with authority and relevance.

The *Inklings on Philosophy and Worldview* book and this guidebook have been carefully designed and developed from over twenty years of teaching this material to produce these tools for continual use as a guide and resource for a lifetime of Christ-centered biblical worldview growth, development, and practice. I owe a special thanks to one of my former students, Tate Fritz, for his tireless and seemingly endless work to help get the first draft of this guidebook started. Almost eight years later, I have the privilege of teaching this class alongside Tate this spring. Like Tate, readers (and those who lead them) are meant to use this book for their own journeys and then as guides to help others through the process.

There are many activities offered in this text that will help readers to further engage with the concepts in the *Inklings on Philosophy and Worldview* book. These activities have been carefully engineered and organized to be effective in a wide variety of learning environments including mentoring and small groups, homeschools and co-schools, and collegiate and traditional high schools. **Learning adventures** are assignments that can be completed right in the guidebook. They are responses to the text and discussions that will help readers to better understand the material. **Extend your learning** activities are designed to get readers outside the book and guidebook and into their world. These require interaction with other texts or media and conversations with other people and will help them make connections between what they're learning and the world they inhabit each day. **Exploring ideas** sections offer readers the opportunity to engage with primary texts— both Scripture and other sources, ancient and modern—that will help them better understand the implications of what they're learning. And finally, **beyond the book** sections extend the material within the *Inklings* *on Philosophy and Worldview* book further, both deeper within topics and broader to subjects not covered in the main text.

Beyond this guidebook, you will find more assignments and resources on InTheTrueMyth.org. Ultimately, your goal will be to design your own course or program in your own flare and style, with your own creative and practical lessons. But the InTheTrueMyth.org website has unit plans, lesson plans, creative assignment ideas, video links, handouts, and slideshow presentations, all for free. Please use these to get started. And as you make the material your own, be sure to share your ideas on the website for others to use.

One of the most important aspects of this curriculum is a focus on love and honor and the necessity of approaching worldview and philosophy with "gentleness and respect," as the apostle Peter puts it. Be sure not to skip past these pages in order to save time or get to the "real lessons" on philosophy. Remember, if we empower young people with knowledge but do not help them to be more loving, we are likely creating "noisy gong[s]" and "clanging cymbal[s]" (1 Corinthians 13:1) rather than loving ambassadors of Christ. Again, on the website, there are plenty of resources available to help you start to build or rebuild a "Kingdom community" for your learning environment. Harnessing the power of words and the language of trust for mentoring, parenting, and teaching is of utmost importance because this is the premise of this entire approach to worldview.

Additionally, an essential component for leading others through this material is to maintain an atmosphere of open inquiry and free will. Readers are ultimately being offered worldview options with informed consent. We as leaders, especially in Christian cultures and subcultures, must remember that Jesus only *invited* people to follow him. Jesus didn't force or coerce people to follow him. He invited people into his worldview and his lifestyle. As parents, pastors, and teachers, we should also be modeling his worldview and inviting our children and students into this. When a decision is forced or coerced, we are going against what Jesus did and does. He never forced anyone; he always invited and always invites us. Jesus defines and models for us our primary pedagogical principle for philosophy and worldview: "Seek and you will find" (Matthew 7:7, NIV). This book is a guidebook to help teachers, parents, and young people alike to keep seeking the Truth, who is Christ. If we keep seeking the Truth, we have been assured that we will find the Truth. Paradoxically and simultaneously, we will also be found by him.

A final word: it has been so rewarding to see the power of this curriculum and vocabulary spread throughout entire communities, especially educational communities all around the globe. The experience at the school where I teach has been exponentially enriched for our students and faculty because our entire faculty and staff have adopted this approach to worldview in all subject areas and extracurricular experiences. James Davis writes, "Integrating philosophy across the curriculum forces instructors and students alike to consider how their entire curriculum fits together. Often students are inadvertently, and perhaps occasionally intentionally, encouraged to see subjects in distinct compartments. . . . Students might see the connection between math and science, but many seem to think that the concerns of English are entirely distinct from history and science. Philosophy can help break down some of these artificial divisions . . . by showing that the 'big questions' are present in all courses."* Seneca helps us see that this concept applies not only to each academic discipline but to all of life, every day! "Philosophy . . . moulds and constructs the soul; it orders our life, guides our conduct, shows us what we should do and what we should leave undone; it sits at the helm and directs our course as we waver amid uncertainties. Without it, no one can live fearlessly or in peace of mind. Countless things that happen every hour call for advice; and such advice is to be sought in philosophy."

You are doing important work. Enjoy the journey.

Matthew Dominguez
DECEMBER 2019

---

* James Davis, "Socrates in Homeroom: A Case Study for Integrating Philosophy across a High School Curriculum," *Teaching Philosophy* 36, no. 3 (2013): 217–38.

Trust and the Nature of Reality

Because of God's tender mercy,
    the morning light from heaven is about
    to break upon us,
to give light to those who sit in darkness
    and in the shadow of death,
    and to guide us to the path of peace.

LUKE 1:78-79

Outline

PART ONE ESSENTIAL QUESTIONS

These questions are essential to our learning and growth for this course of study. They are the focus of part 1 of the *Inklings on Philosophy and Worldview* book and the driving force behind this guidebook. The book, your instruction, the supplemental podcasts (available at IntheTrueMyth.org), and the assignments in this guidebook are all developed to help you answer these questions:

1. Why does philosophy matter?
2. Where am I in my spiritual journey? Where do I want to be?
3. What is the nature of reality?
4. How do humans create a belief system or worldview?
5. What is the suicide of thought? How do I get out of it or help others out of it?
6. What is a philosophical axiom?
7. What is the difference between subjective and objective truth?
8. What is the nature of reality? What is truly real?
9. How does my "trust list" affect my daily decisions and how I interact with others?

PART ONE SUGGESTED READINGS

○ All of part 1 from the *Inklings on Philosophy and Worldview* book (pages 9–50)

○ William E. Brown: "World of Worldviews" (supplemental)

○ Plato: "The Allegory of the Cave" from *The Republic* (pages 22–28)

○ Phillip Yancey: "Prophet of Mirth" (supplemental)

○ Paul: Ephesians (pages 37–48)

○ G. K. Chesterton: "The Suicide of Thought" from *Orthodoxy* (pages 52–70)

PART ONE LEARNING OPPORTUNITIES

Learning Adventures

○ Faith Island and the Trust Lists (pages 8–10)

○ Learning about Big Philosophical Questions in Life: Views of Reality and Core Philosophy (pages 14–18)

○ Notes on Faith, Trust, and Belief: Anna's Pet (page 19–20)

○ Faith Island and the Trust Lists: Identifying "Isms" (page 21)

○ Coming Out of the Cave: A Look at Plato and Scripture (pages 31–34)

○ John 1 and "The Allegory of the Cave" (pages 35–36)

○ "The Suicide of Thought": Choice and Free Will (pages 71–72)

○ How and What to Trust: Personal Connections to Subjective/Objective Truth (pages 80–82)

○ Four Perspectives on Morality: Ethical Dilemmas (pages 89–92)

○ Four Perspectives on Perfection: What Is Perfect? (pages 96–98)

Extend Your Learning

○ "Always Be Prepared . . ." (pages 11–13)

○ Plato's "Allegory of the Cave": A Personal Response (pages 29–30)

○ How and What to Trust: Discussion Starters (pages 83–85)

Exploring Ideas

O "The Allegory of the Cave" from Plato's *Republic* (pages 22–28)
O Ephesians, Faith Island, the Trust List, and the Cave (pages 37–48)
O "The Suicide of Thought" from G. K. Chesterton's *Orthodoxy* (pages 52–70)

Beyond the Book

O How to Read G. K. Chesterton: Three Helpful Metaphors (pages 49–51)
O Philosophical Foundations: Axioms (pages 73–76)
O How and What to Trust: Subjective and Objective Truth (pages 77–79)
O Four Perspectives on Morality (pages 86–88)
O Four Perspectives on Perfection (pages 93–95)
O Reflections on Morality and Perfection (pages 73–76)

Coordinates and Bearings for Learning Adventures: Part One

Part 1 is meant to guide you to the beginning of your spiritual journey: trust. It's important to start a journey at the proper trailhead and with the proper gear. No one will begin climbing an unfamiliar mountain without knowing that he or she is on the right trail and without the appropriate gear. Likewise, to begin your spiritual journey, you need to be equipped to begin at the right trailhead of trust and with the appropriate equipment: honesty, love, honor, and an open mind.

This section of your learning journey will focus on and invite you into . . .

+ Embracing this truth: everything in life is based on trust.
+ Growing in awareness and understanding that everyone and every culture has a "trust list."
+ Knowing there are direct, inescapable, natural consequences for what we trust.
+ Seeing the four basic philosophical "trust lists" for everyone on "Faith Island."

+ Acknowledging and expressing love and honor as essential in a global community of trust.
+ Experiencing Plato's "Allegory of the Cave" as a foundational example of reality and a powerful metaphor for our adventure to "renew our minds."
+ Getting to know G. K. Chesterton as a tour de force of writing and thinking on worldview and philosophy.
+ Successfully navigating people through what Chesterton calls the "suicide of thought."
+ Understanding the concept of philosophical axioms and learning about a few key axioms for this adventure in worldview and philosophy.
+ Becoming more aware of subjective and objective truths.
+ Understanding the categorical differences between the expressions and definitions of perfection and morality between the four worldviews and the natural consequences of these differences.

PART 1 SUMMARY

In part 1, we will look at the common denominator of trust. No matter what "ism" we follow—be it idealism, monism, materialism, theism, or a variation of one of these main four—we are trusting in something. Everything is based on trust. The only way we humans live is to make decisions based on whatever we consider trustworthy, though we differ on the object in which we place our confidence. We give authority to whom and what we trust, and it is essential for us to understand that every decision we make is based on our conclusions regarding the nature of reality.

Faith Island and the Trust Lists

We use what we trust. We give authority to what we trust.

We use what we trust to formulate our conclusions on the nature of reality. What are you using? What should you be using?

Complete this basic trust list:

+ I trust

+ I trust

+ I trust

+ I trust

+ I trust

+ I trust

If you are doing this with a learning group, create a trust list for the rest of the adventure together. What are you as a group going to use to figure out reality?

What are some things or people that are trustworthy?

What makes something or someone trustworthy?

+ We trust

+ We trust

+ We trust

+ We trust

+ We trust

+ We trust

Key concept: If objective truth exists—which it most likely does—we must accept that our access to it is through that which is subjective.

DISCUSSION

Key thought for reflection and discussion: Christians can and should believe in absolute objective truth such as God and the Bible. However, a healthy Christian, Muslim, Hindu, or Buddhist will gladly accept and humbly admit that every person's access to God and the truth presented in their holy texts is through that which is subjective and suspect, such as our perceptions, senses, emotions, brains, or personalities. Everything is based on *trust*!

1. What are the implications of this reality as we approach what we trust in light of what others choose to trust?

2. Considering that there are thousands of Christian denominations, what are the implications of this idea that everything is based on trust within the body of Christ? How does this inform the notion that Christians all over the planet strive for the harmony and unity that Jesus himself prayed for before his death (see John 17)?

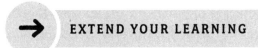
"Always Be Prepared..."

1 Peter 3:15 says, "Always be prepared to give an answer to everyone who asks you to give the reason for the hope that you have. But do this with gentleness and respect" (NIV). Here are some reflection opportunities, discussion questions, and ideas to ponder around this verse.

1. What "answers" to life's tough questions are you looking for? How about your friends? (If you need help thinking of tough questions, consider looking ahead to chapter 7 of the *Inklings on Philosophy and Worldview* book.)

2. Describe some real-life scenarios where you were not prepared to give an answer to life's hard questions. Describe some situations where you were prepared. What were the key differences in these situations? Why were you were prepared in one situation and not the other?

3. Where have you seen in books, videos, movies, lectures, or sermons people who were and were not prepared to answer life's hardest questions? What were the key differences between those who were and were not prepared?

4. Describe some situations where conversations about hard questions were not handled "with gentleness and respect." What was the outcome?

5. Where have you seen in books, videos, movies, lectures, or sermons people who were and were not displaying "gentleness and respect" in tackling the hardest questions of our journeys?

6. Often people will say that an "inclusive approach" to spirituality would work well in answering life's hard questions. They say that the answers are all the same and it does not really matter what religion or belief you pick. In light of the vast differences between the four major worldviews, why does an "inclusive approach" (or pluralistic approach) not actually work? (You may want to see chapter 3 and chapter 5 of *Inklings on Philosophy and Worldview* book if you need a clear picture of the four worldviews and how they are different.)

Learning about Big Philosophical Questions in Life: Views of Reality and Core Philosophy

This activity focuses on the big questions of philosophy, using James Sire's questions from *The Universe Next Door* as a model. I have reworked his questions and reordered them and even added a few of my own. (For a thorough discussion of these questions, see chapter 7 of the *Inklings on Philosophy and Worldview* book, especially pages 63–66.) This is a four-part activity.

Part 1: Write down your answers to these questions today.

Part 2: Revisit and write down your answers after you have studied and pondered part 2 of the guidebook and the *Inklings on Philosophy and Worldview* book.

Part 3: Revisit and write down your answers after studying and pondering part 3 of the guidebook and the *Inklings on Philosophy and Worldview* book.

Part 4: At the end of your study, in a journal-style response, reflect on what stayed the same and what changed. If any of your responses changed, why did you choose to trust different answers to these questions? Make a list of other questions that have come up during your study.

1. What is the nature of reality?

Date: _____ Initial answer:

Date: _____ Response after part 2:

Date: _____ Response after part 3:

2. Who or what is God?

Date: _____ Initial answer:

Date: _____ Response after part 2:

Date: _____ Response after part 3:

3. What is a human being? What is humankind? (Who am I? What am I?)

Date: _____ Initial answer:

Date: _____ Response after part 2:

Date: _____ Response after part 3:

4. What is the basis of and standard for morality? How do I decide between right and wrong, and who or what is the basis for moral authority?

Date: _____ Initial answer:

Date: _____ Response after part 2:

Date: _____ Response after part 3:

5. What happens to humans at death?

Date: _____ Initial answer:

Date: _____ Response after part 2:

Date: _____ Response after part 3:

6. What is the meaning and purpose of human history? What is the essence of human interaction and relationships?

Date: _____ Initial answer:

Date: _____ Response after part 2:

Date: _____ Response after part 3:

7. Why are we here? Where are we going? What is the purpose of human existence?

Date: _____ Initial answer:

Date: _____ Response after part 2:

Date: _____ Response after part 3:

Other questions/responses:

Notes on Faith, Trust, and Belief: Anna's Pet

From the book (page 27):

As an example of how our personal trust lists are shaped by those around us, let's consider a question my daughter Anna asked when she was five years old. Our beloved yellow lab, Pup, had died, and Anna said, "Papa, where did Pup go?" Though she was asking specifically about our dog, she was also indirectly asking what will happen when she dies, when grandpa dies, when her papa dies. It was and is a universal question. . . . Therefore, Anna's question was an important one, and my answer was also very important since she trusts me and has given massive authority to what I think. My answer would influence how she frames the weighty issues of life and death in her unfolding individual story and as a growing member of our immediate community. In many respects our questions and the various answers we all choose to trust are what directly create much of the dramatic tension in this unfolding global story we are all part of writing.

The issue at stake is there are different answers to Anna's question that have very different consequences, and the trust lists of the four major worldviews enable us to navigate this important scenario and others like it.

What would *you* say to Anna at age 5 as she is holding the lifeless body of her beloved pet? "Papa, where did Pup go?"

Faith Island and the Trust Lists: Identifying "Isms"

There are two realms that are a part of every worldview: the spiritual and the material.

There are four distinct views to take on how these two realms form reality. All of the isms, religions, views, tribes, people, and ways are represented within this framework.

Individually or in a group, list as many religions, isms, and ways as you can for each worldview.

S	M	S-M	S+M
Idealism	Materialism	Monism	Theism

"The Allegory of the Cave" from Plato's *Republic*

ANALYZING THE TEXT

The text below is from the Benjamin Jowett translation of *The Republic* by Plato. Written nearly four centuries before Christ, *The Republic* is a dialogue between the philosopher Socrates and various discussion partners about justice and the ideal state. This portion of the dialogue appears in book 7. Socrates discusses the nature of reality with Glaucon, and the dialogue alternates between the two. As you read, underline or highlight at least three passages that interest you or that you would like to bring up during a group discussion. Also create two (or more) questions for group discussion and write them in the margins.

SPACE TO
WRITE OR
DOODLE

THE ALLEGORY OF THE CAVE

[Socrates:] And now, I said, let me show in a figure how far our nature is enlightened or unenlightened: —Behold! human beings living in an underground den, which has a mouth open towards the light and reaching all along the den; here they have been from their childhood, and have their legs and necks chained so that they cannot move, and can only see before them, being prevented by the chains from turning round their heads. Above and behind them a fire is blazing at a distance, and between the fire and the prisoners there is a raised way; and you will see, if you look, a low wall built along the way, like the screen which marionette players have in front of them, over which they show the puppets.

[Glaucon:] I see.

And do you see, I said, men passing along the wall carrying all sorts of vessels, and statues and figures of animals made of wood and stone and various materials, which appear over the wall? Some of them are talking, others silent.

You have shown me a strange image, and they are strange prisoners.

Like ourselves, I replied; and they see only their own shadows, or the shadows of one another, which the fire throws on the opposite wall of the cave?

True, he said; how could they see anything but the shadows if they were never allowed to move their heads?

And of the objects which are being carried in like manner they would only see the shadows?

Yes, he said.

And if they were able to converse with one another, would they not suppose that they were naming what was actually before them?

Very true.

And suppose further that the prison had an echo which came from the other side, would they not be sure to fancy when one of the passers-by spoke that the voice which they heard came from the passing shadow?

No question, he replied.

To them, I said, the truth would be literally nothing but the shadows of the images.

That is certain.

And now look again, and see what will naturally follow if the prisoners are released and disabused of their error. At first, when any of them is liberated and compelled suddenly to stand up and turn his neck round and walk and look towards the light, he will suffer sharp pains; the glare will distress him, and he will be unable to see the realities of which in his former state he had seen the shadows; and then conceive some one saying to him, that what he saw before was an illusion, but that now, when he is approaching nearer to being and his eye is turned towards more real existence, he has a clearer vision,—what will be his reply? And you may further imagine that his instructor is pointing to the objects as they pass and requiring him to name them,—will he not be perplexed? Will he not fancy that the shadows which he formerly saw are truer than the objects which are now shown to him?

Far truer.

And if he is compelled to look straight at the light, will he not have a pain in his eyes which will make him turn away to take refuge in the objects of vision which he can see, and which he will conceive to be in reality clearer than the things which are now being shown to him?

True, he said.

And suppose once more, that he is reluctantly dragged up a steep and rugged ascent, and held fast until he is forced into the presence of the sun himself, is he not likely to be pained and irritated? When he approaches the light his eyes will be dazzled, and he will not be able to see anything at all of what are now called realities.

Not all in a moment, he said.

He will require to grow accustomed to the sight of the upper world. And first he will see the shadows best, next the reflections of men and other objects in the water, and then the objects themselves; then he will gaze upon the light of the moon and the stars and the spangled heaven; and he will see the sky and the stars by night better than the sun or the light of the sun by day?

Certainly.

Last of all he will be able to see the sun, and not mere reflections of him in the water, but he will see him in his own proper place, and not in another; and he will contemplate him as he is.

Certainly.

He will then proceed to argue that this is he who gives the season and the years, and is the guardian of all that is in the visible world, and in a certain way the cause of all things which he and his fellows have been accustomed to behold?

Clearly, he said, he would first see the sun and then reason about him.

And when he remembered his old habitation, and the wisdom of the den and his fellow-prisoners, do you not suppose that he would felicitate himself on the change, and pity them?

Certainly, he would.

And if they were in the habit of conferring honors among themselves on those who were quickest to observe the passing shadows and to remark which of them went before, and which followed after, and which were together; and who were therefore best able to draw conclusions as to the future, do you think that he would care for such honours and glories, or envy the possessors of them? Would he not say with Homer, "Better to be the poor servant of a poor master," and to endure anything, rather than think as they do and live after their manner?

Yes, he said, I think that he would rather suffer anything than entertain these false notions and live in this miserable manner.

Imagine once more, I said, such a one coming suddenly out of the sun to be replaced in his old situation; would he not be certain to have his eyes full of darkness?

To be sure, he said.

And if there were a contest, and he had to compete in measuring the shadows with the prisoners who had never moved out of the den, while his sight was still weak, and before his eyes had become steady (and the time which would be needed to acquire this new habit of sight might be very considerable), would he not be ridiculous? Men would say of him that up he went and down he came without his eyes; and that it was better not even to think of ascending; and if any one tried to loose another and lead him up to the light, let them only catch the offender, and they would put him to death.

No question, he said.

This entire allegory, I said, you may now append, dear Glaucon, to the previous argument; the prison-house is the world of sight, the light of the fire is the sun, and you will not misapprehend me if you interpret the journey upwards to be the ascent of the soul into the intellectual world according to my poor belief, which, at your desire, I have expressed—whether rightly or wrongly God knows. But, whether true or false, my opinion is that in the world of knowledge the idea of good appears last of all, and is seen only with an effort; and, when seen, is also inferred to be the universal author of all things beautiful and right, parent of light and of the lord of light in this visible world, and the immediate source of reason and truth in the intellectual; and that this is the power upon which he who would act rationally either in public or private life must have his eye fixed.

I agree, he said, as far as I am able to understand you.

Moreover, I said, you must not wonder that those who

attain to this beatific vision are unwilling to descend to human affairs; for their souls are ever hastening into the upper world where they desire to dwell; which desire of theirs is very natural, if our allegory may be trusted.

Yes, very natural.

And is there anything surprising in one who passes from divine contemplations to the evil state of man, misbehaving himself in a ridiculous manner; if, while his eyes are blinking and before he has become accustomed to the surrounding darkness, he is compelled to fight in courts of law, or in other places, about the images or the shadows of images of justice, and is endeavouring to meet the conceptions of those who have never yet seen absolute justice?

Anything but surprising, he replied.

Anyone who has common sense will remember that the bewilderments of the eyes are of two kinds, and arise from two causes, either from coming out of the light or from going into the light, which is true of the mind's eye, quite as much as of the bodily eye; and he who remembers this when he sees any one whose vision is perplexed and weak, will not be too ready to laugh; he will first ask whether that soul of man has come out of the brighter life, and is unable to see because unaccustomed to the dark, or having turned from darkness to the day is dazzled by excess light. And he will count the one happy in his condition and state of being, and he will pity the other; or, if he have a mind to laugh at the soul which comes from below into the light, there will be more reason in this than in the laugh which greets him who returns from above out of the light into the den.

That, he said, is a very just distinction.

But then, if I am right, certain professors of education must be wrong when they say that they can put knowledge into the soul which was not there before, like sight into blind eyes.

They undoubtedly say this, he replied.

Whereas, our argument shows that the power and capacity of learning exists in the soul already; and that just as the eye was unable to turn from darkness to light without the whole body, so too the instrument of knowledge can only by the movement of the whole soul be turned from the world of becoming into that of being, and learn by degrees to endure the sight of being, and of the brightness of best of being, or in other words, of the good.*

---

* Translated by Benjamin Jowett.

Plato's "Allegory of the Cave": A Personal Response

1. Write a personal response to the "Allegory of the Cave" reading.

   The realization of the light and the shadows is a good representation for the mysterious and overwhelming God.

2. Working alone or in a group, read carefully through Plato's "Allegory of the Cave" and note all the uses of metaphor, simile, and analogy you can find. This passage is used in education, philosophy, and spiritual formation classes all over the globe. In light of this, how might the metaphors, similes, and analogies you

found be used to help students on their worldview, learning, and spiritual journeys?

EXTEND YOUR LEARNING: Rewrite the allegory of the cave using your friends or relatives, and use the setting, language, and metaphors that fit your group, team, class, or community.

Coming Out of the Cave: A Look at Plato and Scripture

Write a short response to each of the following Scripture passages that highlights its connection to the allegory of the cave. Be prepared for discussion and sharing.

O LORD, you are my lamp. The LORD lights up my darkness.

2 SAMUEL 22:29

He uncovers mysteries hidden in darkness; he brings light to the deepest gloom.

JOB 12:22

They grope in the darkness without a light. He makes them stagger like drunkards.

JOB 12:25

He lit up the way before me and I walked safely through the darkness.

JOB 29:3

You light a lamp for me. The LORD, my God, lights up my darkness.

PSALM 18:28

I could ask the darkness to hide me and the light around me to become night—but even in darkness I cannot hide from you. To you the night shines as bright as day. Darkness and light are the same to you.

PSALM 139:11-12

What sorrow for those who say that evil is good and good is evil, that dark is light and light is dark, that bitter is sweet and sweet is bitter.

ISAIAH 5:20

The people who walk in darkness will see a great light. For those who live in a land of deep darkness, a light will shine.
ISAIAH 9:2

There is no justice among us, and we know nothing about right living. We look for light but find only darkness. We look for bright skies but walk in gloom.
ISAIAH 59:9

When your eye is unhealthy, your whole body is filled with darkness. And if the light you think you have is actually darkness, how deep that darkness is!
MATTHEW 6:23

The judgment is based on this fact: God's light came into the world, but people loved the darkness more than the light, for their actions were evil.
JOHN 3:19

Do everything without complaining and arguing, so that no one can criticize you. Live clean, innocent lives as children of God, shining like bright lights in a world full of crooked and perverse people. Hold firmly to the word of life; then, on the day of Christ's return, I will be proud that I did not run the race in vain and that my work was not useless.

PHILIPPIANS 2:14-16

God, who said, "Let there be light in the darkness," has made this light shine in our hearts so we could know the glory of God that is seen in the face of Jesus Christ.

2 CORINTHIANS 4:6

Jesus spoke to the people once more and said, "I am the light of the world. If you follow me, you won't have to walk in darkness, because you will have the light that leads to life."

JOHN 8:12

John 1 and "The Allegory of the Cave"

Highlight all the connections you can find between "The Allegory of the Cave" and John 1:1-18. Be prepared for discussion and sharing.

¹In the beginning the Word already existed.
    The Word was with God,
    and the Word was God.
²He existed in the beginning with God.
³God created everything through him,
    and nothing was created except through him.
⁴The Word gave life to everything that was created,
    and his life brought light to everyone.
⁵The light shines in the darkness,
    and the darkness can never extinguish it.

⁶God sent a man, John the Baptist, ⁷to tell about the light so that everyone might believe because of his testimony. ⁸John himself was not the light; he was simply a witness to tell about the light. ⁹The one who is the true light, who gives light to everyone, was coming into the world.

[10]He came into the very world he created, but the world didn't recognize him. [11]He came to his own people, and even they rejected him. [12]But to all who believed him and accepted him, he gave the right to become children of God. [13]They are reborn—not with a physical birth resulting from human passion or plan, but a birth that comes from God.

[14]So the Word became human and made his home among us. He was full of unfailing love and faithfulness. And we have seen his glory, the glory of the Father's one and only Son.

[15]John testified about him when he shouted to the crowds, "This is the one I was talking about when I said, 'Someone is coming after me who is far greater than I am, for he existed long before me.'"

[16]From his abundance we have all received one gracious blessing after another. [17]For the law was given through Moses, but God's unfailing love and faithfulness came through Jesus Christ. [18]No one has ever seen God. But the unique One, who is himself God, is near to the Father's heart. He has revealed God to us.

You have to love God more than anything or anyone

In order to love God you have to honor and love Jesus.

Ephesians, Faith Island, the Trust List, and the Cave

ANALYZING THE TEXT

As you read Paul's letter to the Ephesians, consider the connections to belief, trust, faith, Faith Island, trust lists, and Plato's "Allegory of the Cave."

Highlight or underline at least three verses or passages in Ephesians that you find engaging, and be prepared to explain why you picked those verses.

EPHESIANS

Chapter 1

 ¹This letter is from Paul, chosen by the will of God to be an apostle of Christ Jesus.

I am writing to God's holy people in Ephesus, who are faithful followers of Christ Jesus.

²May God our Father and the Lord Jesus Christ give you grace and peace.

³All praise to God, the Father of our Lord Jesus Christ, who has blessed us with every spiritual blessing in the

SPACE TO
WRITE OR
DOODLE

heavenly realms because we are united with Christ. ⁴Even before he made the world, God loved us and chose us in Christ to be holy and without fault in his eyes. ⁵God decided in advance to adopt us into his own family by bringing us to himself through Jesus Christ. This is what he wanted to do, and it gave him great pleasure. ⁶So we praise God for the glorious grace he has poured out on us who belong to his dear Son. ⁷He is so rich in kindness and grace that he purchased our freedom with the blood of his Son and forgave our sins. ⁸He has showered his kindness on us, along with all wisdom and understanding.

⁹God has now revealed to us his mysterious will regarding Christ—which is to fulfill his own good plan. ¹⁰And this is the plan: At the right time he will bring everything together under the authority of Christ—everything in heaven and on earth. ¹¹Furthermore, because we are united with Christ, we have received an inheritance from God, for he chose us in advance, and he makes everything work out according to his plan.

¹²God's purpose was that we Jews who were the first to trust in Christ would bring praise and glory to God. ¹³And now you Gentiles have also heard the truth, the Good News that God saves you. And when you believed in Christ, he identified you as his own by giving you the Holy Spirit, whom he promised long ago. ¹⁴The Spirit is God's guarantee that he will give us the inheritance he promised and that he has purchased us to be his own people. He did this so we would praise and glorify him.

¹⁵Ever since I first heard of your strong faith in the Lord Jesus and your love for God's people everywhere, ¹⁶I have not stopped thanking God for you. I pray for you constantly, ¹⁷asking God, the glorious Father of our Lord Jesus Christ, to give you spiritual wisdom and insight so that you might grow in your knowledge of God. ¹⁸I pray that your

hearts will be flooded with light so that you can understand the confident hope he has given to those he called—his holy people who are his rich and glorious inheritance.

[19]I also pray that you will understand the incredible greatness of God's power for us who believe him. This is the same mighty power [20]that raised Christ from the dead and seated him in the place of honor at God's right hand in the heavenly realms. [21]Now he is far above any ruler or authority or power or leader or anything else—not only in this world but also in the world to come. [22]God has put all things under the authority of Christ and has made him head over all things for the benefit of the church. [23]And the church is his body; it is made full and complete by Christ, who fills all things everywhere with himself.

Chapter 2

[1]Once you were dead because of your disobedience and your many sins. [2]You used to live in sin, just like the rest of the world, obeying the devil—the commander of the powers in the unseen world. He is the spirit at work in the hearts of those who refuse to obey God. [3]All of us used to live that way, following the passionate desires and inclinations of our sinful nature. By our very nature we were subject to God's anger, just like everyone else.

[4]But God is so rich in mercy, and he loved us so much, [5]that even though we were dead because of our sins, he gave us life when he raised Christ from the dead. (It is only by God's grace that you have been saved!) [6]For he raised us from the dead along with Christ and seated us with him in the heavenly realms because we are united with Christ Jesus. [7]So God can point to us in all future ages as examples of the incredible wealth of his grace and kindness toward us, as shown in all he has done for us who are united with Christ Jesus.

⁸God saved you by his grace when you believed. And you can't take credit for this; it is a gift from God. ⁹Salvation is not a reward for the good things we have done, so none of us can boast about it. ¹⁰For we are God's masterpiece. He has created us anew in Christ Jesus, so we can do the good things he planned for us long ago.

¹¹Don't forget that you Gentiles used to be outsiders. You were called "uncircumcised heathens" by the Jews, who were proud of their circumcision, even though it affected only their bodies and not their hearts. ¹²In those days you were living apart from Christ. You were excluded from citizenship among the people of Israel, and you did not know the covenant promises God had made to them. You lived in this world without God and without hope. ¹³But now you have been united with Christ Jesus. Once you were far away from God, but now you have been brought near to him through the blood of Christ.

¹⁴For Christ himself has brought peace to us. He united Jews and Gentiles into one people when, in his own body on the cross, he broke down the wall of hostility that separated us. ¹⁵He did this by ending the system of law with its commandments and regulations. He made peace between Jews and Gentiles by creating in himself one new people from the two groups. ¹⁶Together as one body, Christ reconciled both groups to God by means of his death on the cross, and our hostility toward each other was put to death.

¹⁷He brought this Good News of peace to you Gentiles who were far away from him, and peace to the Jews who were near. ¹⁸Now all of us can come to the Father through the same Holy Spirit because of what Christ has done for us.

¹⁹So now you Gentiles are no longer strangers and foreigners. You are citizens along with all of God's holy

people. You are members of God's family. [20]Together, we are his house, built on the foundation of the apostles and the prophets. And the cornerstone is Christ Jesus himself. [21]We are carefully joined together in him, becoming a holy temple for the Lord. [22]Through him you Gentiles are also being made part of this dwelling where God lives by his Spirit.

Chapter 3

[1]When I think of all this, I, Paul, a prisoner of Christ Jesus for the benefit of you Gentiles . . . [2]assuming, by the way, that you know God gave me the special responsibility of extending his grace to you Gentiles. [3]As I briefly wrote earlier, God himself revealed his mysterious plan to me. [4]As you read what I have written, you will understand my insight into this plan regarding Christ. [5]God did not reveal it to previous generations, but now by his Spirit he has revealed it to his holy apostles and prophets.

[6]And this is God's plan: Both Gentiles and Jews who believe the Good News share equally in the riches inherited by God's children. Both are part of the same body, and both enjoy the promise of blessings because they belong to Christ Jesus. [7]By God's grace and mighty power, I have been given the privilege of serving him by spreading this Good News.

[8]Though I am the least deserving of all God's people, he graciously gave me the privilege of telling the Gentiles about the endless treasures available to them in Christ. [9]I was chosen to explain to everyone this mysterious plan that God, the Creator of all things, had kept secret from the beginning.

[10]God's purpose in all this was to use the church to display his wisdom in its rich variety to all the unseen rulers and authorities in the heavenly places. [11]This was his

eternal plan, which he carried out through Christ Jesus our Lord.

[12]Because of Christ and our faith in him, we can now come boldly and confidently into God's presence. [13]So please don't lose heart because of my trials here. I am suffering for you, so you should feel honored.

[14]When I think of all this, I fall to my knees and pray to the Father, [15]the Creator of everything in heaven and on earth. [16]I pray that from his glorious, unlimited resources he will empower you with inner strength through his Spirit. [17]Then Christ will make his home in your hearts as you trust in him. Your roots will grow down into God's love and keep you strong. [18]And may you have the power to understand, as all God's people should, how wide, how long, how high, and how deep his love is. [19]May you experience the love of Christ, though it is too great to understand fully. Then you will be made complete with all the fullness of life and power that comes from God.

[20]Now all glory to God, who is able, through his mighty power at work within us, to accomplish infinitely more than we might ask or think. [21]Glory to him in the church and in Christ Jesus through all generations forever and ever! Amen.

Chapter 4

[1]Therefore I, a prisoner for serving the Lord, beg you to lead a life worthy of your calling, for you have been called by God. [2]Always be humble and gentle. Be patient with each other, making allowance for each other's faults because of your love. [3]Make every effort to keep yourselves united in the Spirit, binding yourselves together with peace. [4]For there is one body and one Spirit, just as you have been called to one glorious hope for the future.

⁵There is one Lord, one faith, one baptism,
⁶one God and Father of all,

who is over all, in all, and living through all.

⁷However, he has given each one of us a special gift through the generosity of Christ. ⁸That is why the Scriptures say,

"When he ascended to the heights,
he led a crowd of captives
and gave gifts to his people."

⁹Notice that it says "he ascended." This clearly means that Christ also descended to our lowly world. ¹⁰And the same one who descended is the one who ascended higher than all the heavens, so that he might fill the entire universe with himself.

¹¹Now these are the gifts Christ gave to the church: the apostles, the prophets, the evangelists, and the pastors and teachers. ¹²Their responsibility is to equip God's people to do his work and build up the church, the body of Christ. ¹³This will continue until we all come to such unity in our faith and knowledge of God's Son that we will be mature in the Lord, measuring up to the full and complete standard of Christ.

¹⁴Then we will no longer be immature like children. We won't be tossed and blown about by every wind of new teaching. We will not be influenced when people try to trick us with lies so clever they sound like the truth. ¹⁵Instead, we will speak the truth in love, growing in every way more and more like Christ, who is the head of his body, the church. ¹⁶He makes the whole body fit together perfectly. As each part does its own special work, it helps

the other parts grow, so that the whole body is healthy and growing and full of love.

[17]With the Lord's authority I say this: Live no longer as the Gentiles do, for they are hopelessly confused. [18]Their minds are full of darkness; they wander far from the life God gives because they have closed their minds and hardened their hearts against him. [19]They have no sense of shame. They live for lustful pleasure and eagerly practice every kind of impurity.

[20]But that isn't what you learned about Christ. [21]Since you have heard about Jesus and have learned the truth that comes from him, [22]throw off your old sinful nature and your former way of life, which is corrupted by lust and deception. [23]Instead, let the Spirit renew your thoughts and attitudes. [24]Put on your new nature, created to be like God—truly righteous and holy.

[25]So stop telling lies. Let us tell our neighbors the truth, for we are all parts of the same body. [26]And "don't sin by letting anger control you." Don't let the sun go down while you are still angry, [27]for anger gives a foothold to the devil.

[28]If you are a thief, quit stealing. Instead, use your hands for good hard work, and then give generously to others in need. [29]Don't use foul or abusive language. Let everything you say be good and helpful, so that your words will be an encouragement to those who hear them.

[30]And do not bring sorrow to God's Holy Spirit by the way you live. Remember, he has identified you as his own, guaranteeing that you will be saved on the day of redemption.

[31]Get rid of all bitterness, rage, anger, harsh words, and slander, as well as all types of evil behavior. [32]Instead, be kind to each other, tenderhearted, forgiving one another, just as God through Christ has forgiven you.

Chapter 5

[1]Imitate God, therefore, in everything you do, because you are his dear children. [2]Live a life filled with love, following the example of Christ. He loved us and offered himself as a sacrifice for us, a pleasing aroma to God.

[3]Let there be no sexual immorality, impurity, or greed among you. Such sins have no place among God's people. [4]Obscene stories, foolish talk, and coarse jokes—these are not for you. Instead, let there be thankfulness to God. [5]You can be sure that no immoral, impure, or greedy person will inherit the Kingdom of Christ and of God. For a greedy person is an idolater, worshiping the things of this world.

[6]Don't be fooled by those who try to excuse these sins, for the anger of God will fall on all who disobey him. [7]Don't participate in the things these people do. [8]For once you were full of darkness, but now you have light from the Lord. So live as people of light! [9]For this light within you produces only what is good and right and true.

[10]Carefully determine what pleases the Lord. [11]Take no part in the worthless deeds of evil and darkness; instead, expose them. [12]It is shameful even to talk about the things that ungodly people do in secret. [13]But their evil intentions will be exposed when the light shines on them, [14]for the light makes everything visible. This is why it is said,

"Awake, O sleeper,
　　rise up from the dead,
　　and Christ will give you light."

[15]So be careful how you live. Don't live like fools, but like those who are wise. [16]Make the most of every opportunity in these evil days. [17]Don't act thoughtlessly, but understand what the Lord wants you to do. [18]Don't be

drunk with wine, because that will ruin your life. Instead, be filled with the Holy Spirit, [19]singing psalms and hymns and spiritual songs among yourselves, and making music to the Lord in your hearts. [20]And give thanks for everything to God the Father in the name of our Lord Jesus Christ.

[21]And further, submit to one another out of reverence for Christ.

[22]For wives, this means submit to your husbands as to the Lord. [23]For a husband is the head of his wife as Christ is the head of the church. He is the Savior of his body, the church. [24]As the church submits to Christ, so you wives should submit to your husbands in everything.

[25]For husbands, this means love your wives, just as Christ loved the church. He gave up his life for her [26]to make her holy and clean, washed by the cleansing of God's word. [27]He did this to present her to himself as a glorious church without a spot or wrinkle or any other blemish. Instead, she will be holy and without fault. [28]In the same way, husbands ought to love their wives as they love their own bodies. For a man who loves his wife actually shows love for himself. [29]No one hates his own body but feeds and cares for it, just as Christ cares for the church. [30]And we are members of his body.

[31]As the Scriptures say, "A man leaves his father and mother and is joined to his wife, and the two are united into one." [32]This is a great mystery, but it is an illustration of the way Christ and the church are one. [33]So again I say, each man must love his wife as he loves himself, and the wife must respect her husband.

Chapter 6

[1]Children, obey your parents because you belong to the Lord, for this is the right thing to do. [2]"Honor your father

and mother." This is the first commandment with a promise: [3]If you honor your father and mother, "things will go well for you, and you will have a long life on the earth."

[4]Fathers, do not provoke your children to anger by the way you treat them. Rather, bring them up with the discipline and instruction that comes from the Lord.

[5]Slaves, obey your earthly masters with deep respect and fear. Serve them sincerely as you would serve Christ. [6]Try to please them all the time, not just when they are watching you. As slaves of Christ, do the will of God with all your heart. [7]Work with enthusiasm, as though you were working for the Lord rather than for people. [8]Remember that the Lord will reward each one of us for the good we do, whether we are slaves or free.

[9]Masters, treat your slaves in the same way. Don't threaten them; remember, you both have the same Master in heaven, and he has no favorites.

[10]A final word: Be strong in the Lord and in his mighty power. [11]Put on all of God's armor so that you will be able to stand firm against all strategies of the devil. [12]For we are not fighting against flesh-and-blood enemies, but against evil rulers and authorities of the unseen world, against mighty powers in this dark world, and against evil spirits in the heavenly places.

[13]Therefore, put on every piece of God's armor so you will be able to resist the enemy in the time of evil. Then after the battle you will still be standing firm. [14]Stand your ground, putting on the belt of truth and the body armor of God's righteousness. [15]For shoes, put on the peace that comes from the Good News so that you will be fully prepared. [16]In addition to all of these, hold up the shield of faith to stop the fiery arrows of the devil. [17]Put on salvation as your helmet, and take the sword of the Spirit, which is the word of God.

[18]Pray in the Spirit at all times and on every occasion. Stay alert and be persistent in your prayers for all believers everywhere.

[19]And pray for me, too. Ask God to give me the right words so I can boldly explain God's mysterious plan that the Good News is for Jews and Gentiles alike. [20]I am in chains now, still preaching this message as God's ambassador. So pray that I will keep on speaking boldly for him, as I should.

[21]To bring you up to date, Tychicus will give you a full report about what I am doing and how I am getting along. He is a beloved brother and faithful helper in the Lord's work. [22]I have sent him to you for this very purpose—to let you know how we are doing and to encourage you.

[23]Peace be with you, dear brothers and sisters, and may God the Father and the Lord Jesus Christ give you love with faithfulness. [24]May God's grace be eternally upon all who love our Lord Jesus Christ.

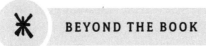

How to Read
G. K. Chesterton:
Three Helpful Metaphors

G. K. Chesterton's writing is often difficult to comprehend. While reading *Orthodoxy* for the first time, you may not understand the value of certain passages or wording. When the same words are read years later, the earlier exposure will help build deeper meaning and understanding.

Three metaphors may help you understand his writing better. Western culture trains us to think, read, and write linearly—like a train. The thesis statement is the engine, the evidence and arguments that support the thesis are the boxcars, and the conclusion is the caboose. This sort of writing makes sense to most of us. Although Chesterton is a Western thinker, he does not write linearly, and if you try to read him this way, you might get discouraged. Here are some metaphors to explain how Chesterton writes.

CONSTELLATIONAL WRITING

Chesterton will often make an insightful point over here, then move on to another image over there, and over there is still another idea. His unfolding ideas are seemingly unconnected, yet if you allow him to lead

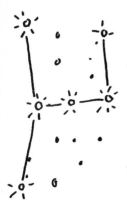

you through the chapter, he ends by helping you step back and see a constellation. Look for the dots, note them as you read, leave them be, and at the end, you will say, "Oh! It is Orion!" Keep in mind that if you try to piece it together on your own, you might naturally be left confused. If you try to force the reading, I can almost guarantee that it will be very confusing. Just read, and then at the end of the chapter, you will be given the bigger picture.

MAKING A STEW

In a seven-course meal, you make and serve each piece separately; you don't mix them all together. With stew, you take all the ingredients and throw them in a big pot. You stir everything up, warm it, and maybe even let it sit for some time. Then at the end it tastes delicious with all the flavors blended together. If you read Chesterton and try to digest his writing as you go (figure it out linearly), it would be like shoving celery salt, then raw meat, then carrots into your mouth; it will be confusing and might not taste good. Relax a bit, and don't try to figure his writing out linearly. Add the ingredients into the Crock-Pot of your mind as you go and let the concepts simmer . . . maybe even let them sit and cook for a few hours. Then take a taste.

PANNING FOR GOLD

The last metaphor for reading Chesterton's writings is panning for gold. Start scooping through his words and sifting, and keep going until something sticks out like gold in your pan. You may or may not have trouble reading him; you may totally enjoy his writing and want to dig into it deeply. Either way, you don't need to understand all of it, but what you do understand will be worth it. I can almost guarantee you that you will find some gold nuggets of truth that can and will last a lifetime. Words are powerful. Truth is powerful. Take the time to look for some powerful, witty words of truth in Chesterton.

> There are an infinity of angles at which one falls, only one at which one stands.
> G. K. CHESTERTON

Here are a few thoughts on G. K. Chesterton from chapter 3 of Philip Yancey's book *Soul Survivor*.

> When someone asked Chesterton what one book he would want to have along if stranded on a desert island, he paused only an instant before replying, "Why, *A Practical Guide to Shipbuilding*, of course." If I were so stranded, and could choose one book apart from the Bible, I may well select Chesterton's own spiritual autobiography, *Orthodoxy*. Why anyone would pick up a book with that formidable title eludes me, but one day I did so and my faith has never recovered. . . .
>
> The churches I attended had stressed the dangers of pleasure so loudly that I had missed any positive message. Guided by Chesterton, I came to see sex, money, power, and sensory pleasures as God's good gifts. . . . Of course, in a world estranged from God, even good things must be handled with care, like explosives. We have lost the untainted innocence of Eden, and every good harbors risk as well, holding within it the potential for abuse. Eating becomes gluttony, love becomes lust, and along the way we lose sight of the One who gave us pleasure.
>
> Chesterton himself said that the modern age is characterized by a sadness that calls for a new kind of prophet, not like prophets of old who reminded people that they were going to die, but someone who would remind them they are not dead yet.

"The Suicide of Thought" from G. K. Chesterton's *Orthodoxy*

ANALYZING THE TEXT

The full text for chapter 3 of G. K. Chesterton's book *Orthodoxy*, "The Suicide of Thought," is included below. As you read "The Suicide of Thought," highlight or underline at least three passages that you find engaging, and be prepared to briefly explain why you picked those passages. Be sure to annotate the text as you read: highlight interesting passages, write down any questions you have, and mark points of particular agreement or disagreement.

SPACE TO
WRITE OR
DOODLE

THE SUICIDE OF THOUGHT

The phrases of the street are not only forcible but subtle: for a figure of speech can often get into a crack too small for a definition. Phrases like "put out" or "off colour" might have been coined by Mr. Henry James in an agony of verbal precision. And there is no more subtle truth than that of the everyday phrase about a man having "his heart in the right place." It involves the idea of normal proportion; not only does a certain function exist, but it is rightly related to other functions. Indeed, the negation of this phrase would describe with peculiar accuracy the somewhat morbid mercy and perverse tenderness of the most representative moderns. If, for instance, I had to describe with fairness the character of Mr. Bernard Shaw, I could not express myself more exactly than by saying that he has a heroically large and generous heart; but not a heart in the right place. And this is so of the typical society of our time.

The modern world is not evil; in some ways the modern world is far too good. It is full of wild and wasted virtues. When a religious scheme is shattered (as Christianity was shattered at the Reformation), it is not merely the vices that are let loose. The vices are, indeed, let loose, and they wander and do damage. But the virtues are let loose also; and the virtues wander more wildly, and the virtues do more terrible damage. The modern world is full of the old Christian virtues gone mad. The virtues have gone mad because they have been isolated from each other and are wandering alone. Thus some scientists care for truth; and their truth is pitiless. Thus some humanitarians only care for pity; and their pity (I am sorry to say) is often untruthful. For example, Mr. Blatchford attacks Christianity because he is mad on one Christian virtue: the merely mystical and almost irrational virtue of charity. He has a strange idea that he will make it easier to forgive sins by saying that there are no sins to forgive. Mr. Blatchford is not only an early Christian, he is the only early Christian who ought really to have been eaten by lions. For in his case the pagan accusation is really true: his mercy would mean mere anarchy. He really is the enemy of the human race—because he is so human. As the other extreme, we may take the acrid realist, who has deliberately killed in himself all human pleasure in happy tales or in the healing of the heart. Torquemada tortured people physically for the sake of moral truth. Zola tortured people morally for the sake of physical truth. But in Torquemada's time there was at least a system that could to some extent make righteousness and peace kiss each other. Now they do not even bow. But a much stronger case than these two of truth and pity can be found in the remarkable case of the dislocation of humility.

It is only with one aspect of humility that we are here concerned. Humility was largely meant as a restraint upon the arrogance and infinity of the appetite of man. He was always outstripping his mercies with his own newly invented needs. His very power of enjoyment destroyed half his joys. By asking for pleasure, he lost the chief pleasure; for the chief pleasure is surprise. Hence it became evident that if a man would make his world large, he must be always making himself small. Even the haughty visions, the tall cities, and the toppling pinnacles are the creations of humility. Giants that tread down forests like grass are the creations of humility. Towers that vanish upwards above the loneliest star are the creations of humility. For towers are not tall unless we look up at them; and giants are not giants unless they are larger than we. All this gigantesque imagination, which is, perhaps, the mightiest of the pleasures of man, is at bottom entirely humble. It is impossible without humility to enjoy anything—even pride.

But what we suffer from to-day is humility in the wrong place. Modesty has moved from the organ of ambition. Modesty has settled upon the organ of conviction; where it was never meant to be. A man was meant to be doubtful about himself, but undoubting about the truth; this has been exactly reversed. Nowadays the part of a man that a man does assert is exactly the part he ought not to assert—himself. The part he doubts is exactly the part he ought not to doubt—the Divine Reason. Huxley preached a humility content to learn from Nature. But the new sceptic is so humble that he doubts if he can even learn. Thus we should be wrong if we had said hastily that there is no humility typical of our time. The truth is that there is a real humility typical of our time; but it so happens that it is practically a more poisonous humility than the wildest prostrations of the ascetic. The old humility was a spur that prevented a man from stopping; not a nail in his boot that prevented him from going on. For the old humility made a man doubtful about his efforts, which might make him work harder. But the new humility makes a man doubtful about his aims, which will make him stop working altogether.

At any street corner we may meet a man who utters the frantic and blasphemous statement that he may be wrong. Every day one comes across somebody who says that of course his view may not be the right one. Of course his view must be the right one, or it is not his view. We are on the road to producing a race of men too mentally modest to believe in the multiplication table. We are in danger of seeing philosophers who doubt the law of gravity as being a mere fancy of their own. Scoffers of old time were too proud to be convinced; but these are too humble to be convinced. The meek do inherit the earth; but the modern sceptics are too meek even to claim their inheritance. It is exactly this intellectual helplessness which is our second problem.

The last chapter has been concerned only with a fact of observation: that what peril of morbidity there is for man comes rather from his reason than his imagination. It was not meant to attack the authority of reason; rather it is the ultimate purpose to defend it. For it needs defence. The whole modern world is at war with reason; and the tower already reels.

The sages, it is often said, can see no answer to the riddle of religion. But the trouble with our sages is not that they cannot see the answer; it is that they cannot even see the riddle. They are like children so stupid as to notice nothing paradoxical in the playful assertion that a door is not a door. The modern latitudinarians speak, for instance, about authority in religion not only as if there were no reason in it, but as if there had never been any reason for it. Apart from seeing its philosophical basis, they cannot even see its historical cause. Religious authority has often, doubtless, been oppressive or unreasonable; just as every legal system (and especially our present one) has been callous and full of a cruel apathy. It is rational to attack the police; nay, it is glorious. But the modern critics of religious authority are like men who should attack the police without ever having heard of burglars. For there is a great and possible peril to the human mind: a peril as practical as burglary. Against it religious authority was reared, rightly or wrongly, as a barrier. And against it something certainly must be reared as a barrier, if our race is to avoid ruin.

That peril is that the human intellect is free to destroy itself. Just as one generation could prevent the very existence of the next generation, by all entering a monastery or jumping into the sea, so one set of thinkers can in some degree prevent further thinking by teaching the next generation that there is no validity in any human thought. It is idle to talk always of the alternative of reason and faith. Reason is itself a matter of faith. It is an act of faith to assert that our thoughts have any relation to reality at all. If you are merely a sceptic, you must sooner or later ask yourself the question, "Why should *anything* go right; even observation and deduction? Why should not good logic be as misleading as bad logic? They are both movements in the brain of a bewildered ape?" The young sceptic says, "I have a right to think for myself." But the old sceptic, the complete sceptic, says, "I have no right to think for myself. I have no right to think at all."

There is a thought that stops thought. That is the only thought that ought to be stopped. That is the ultimate evil against which all religious authority was aimed. It only appears at the end of decadent ages like our own: and already Mr. H.G. Wells has raised its ruinous banner; he has written a delicate piece of scepticism called "Doubts of the Instrument." In this he questions the brain itself, and endeavours to remove all reality from all his own assertions, past, present, and to come. But it was against this remote ruin that all the military systems in religion were originally ranked and ruled. The creeds and the crusades, the hierarchies and the horrible persecutions were not organized, as is ignorantly said, for the suppression of reason. They were organized for the difficult defence of reason. Man, by a blind instinct, knew that if once things were wildly questioned, reason could be questioned first. The authority of priests to absolve, the authority of popes to define the authority, even of inquisitors to terrify: these were all only dark defences erected round one central authority, more undemonstrable, more supernatural than all—the authority of a man to think. We know now that this is so; we have no excuse for not knowing it. For we can hear scepticism crashing through the old ring of authorities, and at the same moment we can see reason swaying upon her throne. In so far as religion is gone, reason is going. For they are both of the same primary and authoritative kind. They are both methods of proof which cannot themselves be proved. And in the act of destroying the idea of Divine authority we have largely destroyed the idea of that human authority by which we do a long-division sum. With a long and sustained tug we have attempted to pull the mitre off pontifical man; and his head has come off with it.

Lest this should be called loose assertion, it is perhaps desirable, though dull, to run rapidly through the chief modern fashions of thought which have this effect of stopping thought itself. Materialism and the view of everything as a personal illusion have some such effect; for if the mind is mechanical, thought cannot be very exciting, and if the cosmos is unreal, there is nothing to think about. But in these cases the effect is indirect and doubtful. In some cases it is direct and clear; notably in the case of what is generally called evolution.

Evolution is a good example of that modern intelligence which, if it destroys anything, destroys itself. Evolution is either an innocent scientific description of how certain earthly things came about; or, if it is anything more than this, it is an attack upon thought itself. If evolution destroys anything, it does not destroy religion but rationalism. If evolution simply means that a positive thing called an ape turned very slowly into a positive thing called a man, then it is stingless for the most orthodox; for a personal God might just as well do things slowly as quickly, especially if, like the Christian God, he were outside time. But if it means anything more, it means that there is no such thing as an ape to change, and no such thing as a man for him to change into. It means that there is no such thing as a thing. At best, there is only one thing, and that is a flux of everything and anything. This is an attack not upon the faith, but upon the mind; you cannot think if there are no things to think about. You cannot think if you are not separate from the subject of thought. Descartes said, "I think; therefore I am." The philosophic evolutionist reverses and negatives the epigram. He says, "I am not; therefore I cannot think."

Then there is the opposite attack on thought: that urged by Mr. H.G. Wells when he insists that every separate thing is "unique," and there are no categories at all. This also is merely destructive. Thinking means connecting things, and stops if they cannot be connected. It need hardly be said that this scepticism forbidding thought necessarily forbids speech; a man cannot open his mouth without contradicting it. Thus when Mr. Wells says (as he did somewhere), "All chairs are quite different," he utters not merely a misstatement, but a contradiction in terms. If all chairs were quite different, you could not call them "all chairs."

Akin to these is the false theory of progress, which maintains that we alter the test instead of trying to pass the test. We often hear it said, for instance, "What is right in one age is wrong in another." This is quite reasonable, if it means that there is a fixed aim, and that certain methods attain at certain times and not at other times. If women, say, desire to be elegant, it may be that they are improved at one time by growing fatter and at another time by growing thinner. But you cannot say that they are improved by ceasing to wish to be elegant and beginning to wish to be oblong. If the standard changes, how can there be improvement, which implies a standard? Nietzsche started a nonsensical idea that men had once sought as good what we now call evil; if it were so, we could not talk of surpassing or even falling short of them. How can you overtake Jones if you walk in the other direction? You cannot discuss whether one people has succeeded more in being miserable than another succeeded in being happy. It would be like discussing whether Milton was more puritanical than a pig is fat.

It is true that a man (a silly man) might make change itself his object or ideal. But as an ideal, change itself becomes unchangeable. If the change-worshipper wishes to estimate his own progress, he must be sternly loyal to the ideal of change; he must not begin to flirt gaily with the ideal of monotony. Progress itself cannot progress. It is worth remark, in passing, that when Tennyson, in a wild and rather weak manner, welcomed the idea of infinite alteration in society, he instinctively took a metaphor which suggests an imprisoned tedium. He wrote—

"Let the great world spin for ever down the ringing grooves of change."

He thought of change itself as an unchangeable groove; and so it is. Change is about the narrowest and hardest groove that a man can get into.

The main point here, however, is that this idea of a fundamental alteration in the standard is one of the things that make thought about the past or future simply impossible. The theory of a complete change of standards in human history does not merely deprive us of the pleasure of honouring our fathers; it deprives us even of the more modern and aristocratic pleasure of despising them.

This bald summary of the thought-destroying forces of our time would not be complete without some reference to pragmatism; for though I have here used and should everywhere defend the pragmatist method as a preliminary guide to truth, there is an extreme application of it which involves the absence of all truth whatever. My meaning can be put shortly thus. I agree with the pragmatists that apparent objective truth is not the whole matter; that there is an authoritative need to believe the things that are necessary to the human mind. But I say that one of those necessities precisely is a belief in objective truth. The pragmatist tells a man to think what he must think and never mind the Absolute. But precisely one of the things that he must think is the Absolute. This philosophy, indeed, is a kind of verbal paradox. Pragmatism is a matter of human needs; and one of the first of human needs is to be something more than a pragmatist. Extreme pragmatism is just as inhuman as the determinism it so powerfully attacks. The determinist (who, to do him justice, does not pretend to be a human being) makes nonsense of the human sense of actual choice. The pragmatist, who professes to be specially human, makes nonsense of the human sense of actual fact.

To sum up our contention so far, we may say that the most characteristic current philosophies have not only a touch of mania, but a touch of suicidal mania. The mere questioner has knocked his head against the limits of human thought; and cracked it. This is what makes so futile the warnings of the orthodox and the boasts of the advanced about the dangerous boyhood of free thought. What we are looking at is not the boyhood of free thought; it is the old age and ultimate dissolution of free thought. It is vain for bishops and pious bigwigs to discuss what dreadful things will happen if wild scepticism runs its course. It has run its course. It is vain for eloquent atheists to talk of the great truths that will be revealed if once we see free thought begin. We have seen it end. It has no more questions to ask; it has questioned itself. You cannot call up any wilder vision than a city in which men ask themselves if they have any selves. You cannot fancy a more sceptical world than that in which men doubt if there is a world. It might certainly have reached its bankruptcy more quickly and cleanly if it had not been feebly hampered by the application of indefensible laws of blasphemy or by the absurd pretence that modern England is Christian. But it would have reached the bankruptcy anyhow. Militant atheists are still unjustly persecuted; but rather because they are an old minority than because they are a new one. Free thought has exhausted its own freedom. It is weary of its own success. If any eager freethinker now hails philosophic freedom as the dawn, he is only like the man in Mark Twain who came out wrapped in blankets to see the sun rise and was just in time to see it set. If any frightened curate still says that it will be awful if the darkness of free thought should spread, we can only answer him in the high and powerful words of Mr. Belloc, "Do not, I beseech you, be troubled about the increase of forces already in dissolution. You have mistaken the hour of the night: it is already morning." We have no more questions left to ask. We have looked for questions in the darkest corners and on the wildest peaks. We have found all the questions that can be found. It is time we gave up looking for questions and began looking for answers.

But one more word must be added. At the beginning of this preliminary negative sketch I said that our mental ruin has been wrought by wild reason, not by wild imagination. A man does not go mad because he makes a statue a mile high, but he may go mad by thinking it out in square inches. Now, one school of thinkers has seen this and jumped at it as a way of renewing the pagan health of the world. They see that reason destroys; but Will, they say, creates. The ultimate authority, they say, is in will, not in reason. The supreme point is not why a man demands a thing, but the fact that he does demand it. I have no space to trace or expound this philosophy of Will. It came, I suppose, through Nietzsche, who preached something that is called egoism. That, indeed, was simpleminded enough; for Nietzsche denied egoism simply by preaching it. To preach anything is to give it away. First, the egoist calls life a war without mercy, and then he takes the greatest possible trouble to drill his enemies in war. To preach egoism is to practise altruism. But however it began, the view is common enough in current literature. The main defence of these thinkers is that they are not thinkers; they are makers. They say that choice is itself the divine thing. Thus Mr. Bernard Shaw has attacked the old idea that men's acts are to be judged by the standard of the desire of happiness. He says that a man does not act for his happiness, but from his will. He does not say, "Jam will make me happy," but "I want jam." And in all this others follow him with yet greater enthusiasm. Mr. John Davidson, a remarkable poet, is so passionately excited about it that he is obliged to write prose. He publishes a short play with several long prefaces. This is natural enough in Mr. Shaw, for all his plays are prefaces: Mr. Shaw is (I suspect) the only man on earth who has never written any poetry. But that Mr. Davidson (who can write excellent poetry) should write instead laborious metaphysics in defence of this doctrine of will, does show that the doctrine of will has taken hold of men. Even Mr. H.G. Wells has half spoken in its language; saying that one should test acts not like a thinker, but like an artist, saying, "I *feel* this curve is right," or "that line *shall* go thus." They are all excited; and well they may be. For by this doctrine of the divine authority of will, they think they can break out of the doomed fortress of rationalism. They think they can escape.

But they cannot escape. This pure praise of volition ends in the same break up and blank as the mere pursuit of logic. Exactly as complete free thought involves the doubting of thought itself, so the acceptation of mere "willing" really paralyzes the will. Mr. Bernard Shaw has not perceived the real difference between the old utilitarian test of pleasure (clumsy, of course, and easily misstated) and that which he propounds. The real difference between the test of happiness and the test of will is simply that the test of happiness is a test and the other isn't. You can discuss whether a man's act in jumping over a cliff was directed towards happiness; you cannot discuss whether it was derived from will. Of course it was. You can praise an action by saying that it is calculated to bring pleasure or pain to discover truth or to save the soul. But you cannot praise an action because it shows will;

for to say that is merely to say that it is an action. By this praise of will you cannot really choose one course as better than another. And yet choosing one course as better than another is the very definition of the will you are praising.

The worship of will is the negation of will. To admire mere choice is to refuse to choose. If Mr. Bernard Shaw comes up to me and says, "Will something," that is tantamount to saying, "I do not mind what you will," and that is tantamount to saying, "I have no will in the matter." You cannot admire will in general, because the essence of will is that it is particular. A brilliant anarchist like Mr. John Davidson feels an irritation against ordinary morality, and therefore he invokes will—will to anything. He only wants humanity to want something. But humanity does want something. It wants ordinary morality. He rebels against the law and tells us to will something or anything. But we have willed something. We have willed the law against which he rebels.

All the will-worshippers, from Nietzsche to Mr. Davidson, are really quite empty of volition. They cannot will, they can hardly wish. And if any one wants a proof of this, it can be found quite easily. It can be found in this fact: that they always talk of will as something that expands and breaks out. But it is quite the opposite. Every act of will is an act of self-limitation. To desire action is to desire limitation. In that sense every act is an act of self-sacrifice. When you choose anything, you reject everything else. That objection, which men of this school used to make to the act of marriage, is really an objection to every act. Every act is an irrevocable selection and exclusion. Just as when you marry one woman you give up all the others, so when you take one course of action you give up all the other courses. If you become King of England, you give up the post of Beadle in Brompton. If you go to Rome, you sacrifice a rich suggestive life in Wimbledon. It is the existence of this negative or limiting side of will that makes most of the talk of the anarchic will-worshippers little better than nonsense. For instance, Mr. John Davidson tells us to have nothing to do with "Thou shalt not"; but it is surely obvious that "Thou shalt not" is only one of the necessary corollaries of "I will." "I will go to the Lord Mayor's Show, and thou shalt not stop me." Anarchism adjures us to be bold creative artists, and care for no laws or limits. But it is impossible to be an artist and not care for laws and limits. Art is limitation; the essence of every picture is the frame. If you draw a giraffe, you must draw him with a long neck. If, in your bold creative way, you hold yourself free to draw a giraffe with a short neck, you will really find that you are not free to draw a giraffe. The moment you step into the world of facts, you step into a world of limits. You can free things from alien or accidental laws, but not from the laws of their own nature. You may, if you like, free a tiger from his bars; but do not free him from his stripes. Do not free a camel of the burden of his hump: you may be freeing him from being a camel. Do not go about as a demagogue, encouraging triangles to break out of the prison of their three sides. If a triangle breaks out of its three sides, its life comes to a lamentable end. Somebody wrote a work called "The Loves of the Triangles"; I never read it, but I am sure that if triangles ever were loved, they were loved for being triangular. This is certainly the case with all artistic creation, which is in some ways the most decisive example of pure will. The artist loves his limitations: they constitute the *thing* he is doing. The painter is glad that the canvas is flat. The sculptor is glad that the clay is colourless.

In case the point is not clear, an historic example may illustrate it. The French Revolution was really an heroic and decisive thing, because the Jacobins willed something definite and limited. They desired the freedoms of democracy, but also all the vetoes of democracy. They wished to have votes and *not* to have titles. Republicanism had an ascetic side in Franklin or Robespierre as well as an expansive side in Danton or Wilkes. Therefore they have created something with a solid substance and shape, the square social equality and peasant wealth of France. But since then the revolutionary or speculative mind of Europe has been weakened by shrinking from any proposal because of the limits of that proposal. Liberalism has been degraded into liberality. Men have tried to turn "revolutionise" from a transitive to an intransitive verb. The Jacobin could tell you not only the system he would rebel against, but (what was more important) the system he would *not* rebel against, the system he would trust. But the new rebel is a Sceptic, and will not entirely trust anything. He has no loyalty; therefore he can never be really a revolutionist. And the fact that he doubts everything really gets in his way when he wants to denounce anything. For all denunciation implies a moral doctrine of some kind; and the modern revolutionist doubts not only the institution he denounces, but the doctrine by which he denounces it. Thus he writes one book complaining that imperial oppression insults the purity of women, and then he writes another book (about the sex problem) in which he insults it himself. He curses the Sultan because Christian girls lose their virginity, and then curses Mrs. Grundy because they keep it. As a politician, he will cry out that war is a waste of life, and then, as a philosopher, that all life is waste of time. A Russian pessimist will denounce a policeman for killing a peasant, and then prove by the highest philosophical principles that the peasant ought to have killed himself. A man denounces marriage as a lie, and then denounces aristocratic profligates for treating it as a lie. He calls a flag a bauble, and then blames the oppressors of Poland or Ireland because they take away that bauble. The man of this school goes first to a political meeting, where he complains that savages are treated as if they were beasts; then he takes his hat and umbrella and goes on to a scientific meeting, where he proves that they practically are beasts. In short, the modern revolutionist, being an infinite sceptic, is always engaged in undermining his own mines. In his book on politics he attacks men for trampling on morality; in his book on ethics he attacks morality for trampling on men. Therefore the modern man in revolt has become practically useless for all purposes of revolt. By rebelling against everything he has lost his right to rebel against anything.

It may be added that the same blank and bankruptcy can be observed in all fierce and terrible types of literature, especially in satire. Satire may be mad and anarchic, but it presupposes an admitted superiority in certain things over others; it presupposes a standard. When little boys in the street laugh at the fatness of some distinguished journalist, they are unconsciously assuming a standard of Greek sculpture. They are appealing to the marble Apollo. And the curious disappearance of satire from our literature is an instance of the fierce things fading for want of any principle to be fierce about. Nietzsche had some natural talent for sarcasm: he could sneer, though he could not laugh; but there is always something bodiless and without weight in his satire, simply because it has not any mass of common morality behind it. He is himself more preposterous than anything he denounces. But, indeed, Nietzsche will stand very well as the type of the whole of this failure of abstract violence. The softening of the brain which ultimately overtook him was not a physical accident. If Nietzsche had not ended in imbecility, Nietzscheism would end in imbecility. Thinking in isolation and with pride ends in being an idiot.

Every man who will not have softening of the heart must at last have softening of the brain.

This last attempt to evade intellectualism ends in intellectualism, and therefore in death. The sortie has failed. The wild worship of lawlessness and the materialist worship of law end in the same void. Nietzsche scales staggering mountains, but he turns up ultimately in Tibet. He sits down beside Tolstoy in the land of nothing and Nirvana. They are both helpless—one because he must not grasp anything, and the other because he must not let go of anything. The Tolstoyan's will is frozen by a Buddhist instinct that all special actions are evil. But the Nietzscheite's will is quite equally frozen by his view that all special actions are good; for if all special actions are good, none of them are special. They stand at the crossroads, and one hates all the roads and the other likes all the roads. The result is—well, some things are not hard to calculate. They stand at the cross-roads.

Here I end (thank God) the first and dullest business of this book—the rough review of recent thought. After this I begin to sketch a view of life which may not interest my reader, but which, at any rate, interests me. In front of me, as I close this page, is a pile of modern books that I have been turning over for the purpose—a pile of ingenuity, a pile of futility. By the accident of my present detachment, I can see the inevitable smash of the philosophies of Schopenhauer and Tolstoy, Nietzsche and Shaw, as clearly as an inevitable railway smash could be seen from a balloon. They are all on the road to the emptiness of the asylum. For madness may be defined as using mental activity so as to reach mental helplessness; and they have nearly reached it. He who thinks he is made of glass, thinks to the destruction of thought; for glass cannot think. So he who wills to reject nothing, wills the destruction of will;

for will is not only the choice of something, but the rejec-
tion of almost everything. And as I turn and tumble over
the clever, wonderful, tiresome, and useless modern books,
the title of one of them rivets my eye. It is called "Jeanne
d'Arc," by Anatole France. I have only glanced at it, but a
glance was enough to remind me of Renan's "Vie de Jesus."
It has the same strange method of the reverent sceptic. It
discredits supernatural stories that have some foundation,
simply by telling natural stories that have no foundation.
Because we cannot believe in what a saint did, we are to
pretend that we know exactly what he felt. But I do not
mention either book in order to criticise it, but because the
accidental combination of the names called up two star-
tling images of Sanity which blasted all the books before
me. Joan of Arc was not stuck at the cross-roads, either by
rejecting all the paths like Tolstoy, or by accepting them all
like Nietzsche. She chose a path, and went down it like a
thunderbolt. Yet Joan, when I came to think of her, had in
her all that was true either in Tolstoy or Nietzsche, all that
was even tolerable in either of them. I thought of all that
is noble in Tolstoy, the pleasure in plain things, especially
in plain pity, the actualities of the earth, the reverence for
the poor, the dignity of the bowed back. Joan of Arc had all
that and with this great addition, that she endured poverty
as well as admiring it; whereas Tolstoy is only a typical aris-
tocrat trying to find out its secret. And then I thought of all
that was brave and proud and pathetic in poor Nietzsche,
and his mutiny against the emptiness and timidity of our
time. I thought of his cry for the ecstatic equilibrium of
danger, his hunger for the rush of great horses, his cry to
arms. Well, Joan of Arc had all that, and again with this
difference, that she did not praise fighting, but fought. We
know that she was not afraid of an army, while Nietzsche,
for all we know, was afraid of a cow. Tolstoy only praised

the peasant; she was the peasant. Nietzsche only praised the warrior; she was the warrior. She beat them both at their own antagonistic ideals; she was more gentle than the one, more violent than the other. Yet she was a perfectly practical person who did something, while they are wild speculators who do nothing. It was impossible that the thought should not cross my mind that she and her faith had perhaps some secret of moral unity and utility that has been lost. And with that thought came a larger one, and the colossal figure of her Master had also crossed the theatre of my thoughts. The same modern difficulty which darkened the subject-matter of Anatole France also darkened that of Ernest Renan. Renan also divided his hero's pity from his hero's pugnacity. Renan even represented the righteous anger at Jerusalem as a mere nervous breakdown after the idyllic expectations of Galilee. As if there were any inconsistency between having a love for humanity and having a hatred for inhumanity! Altruists, with thin, weak voices, denounce Christ as an egoist. Egoists (with even thinner and weaker voices) denounce Him as an altruist. In our present atmosphere such cavils are comprehensible enough. The love of a hero is more terrible than the hatred of a tyrant. The hatred of a hero is more generous than the love of a philanthropist. There is a huge and heroic sanity of which moderns can only collect the fragments. There is a giant of whom we see only the lopped arms and legs walking about. **They have torn the soul of Christ into silly strips, labelled egoism and altruism, and they are equally puzzled by His insane magnificence and His insane meekness. They have parted His garments among them, and for His vesture they have cast lots; though the coat was without seam woven from the top throughout.**

"The Suicide of Thought": Choice and Free Will

Chesterton writes, "There is a thought that stops thought. That is the only thought that ought to be stopped." Answer these questions about "The Suicide of Thought."

1. What is the suicide of thought?

2. How does someone get into the suicide of thought?

3. How does someone get out of the suicide of thought?

4. How does free will help us navigate this issue of the suicide of thought?

5. What negative and destructive thoughts could you choose to stop trusting? What powerful truths that bring hope and freedom could you choose to fully trust in order to replace these thoughts?

6. What novels, short stories, or movies incorporate the suicide of thought? How do the characters navigate these questions in the story? Discuss this in the context of how Chesterton addresses the issue. Use chapter 4 of the *Inklings on Philosophy and Worldview* book to help you navigate these discussions.

EXTEND YOUR LEARNING: Create a verbal, written, or video conversation that incorporates the questions above.

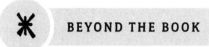

Philosophical Foundations: Axioms

> The stage is set with piles of bricks and stones. Construction materials are strewn about. A half-finished frame, recognizable as the skeleton of a house, looms in the background. A huge hole has been dug into the earth ready for a strong foundation.

Axioms are the foundations on which we build our philosophical houses. They are the pillars or rocks on which we build our daily lives. These statements of truth are often the basement of our thinking and living, hidden underground. They are in fact essential because everything is resting on them. If they are faulty, the whole house is unstable. Thus, an axiom must be self-evident and irrefutable. A solid foundation gives stability and confidence to a solid house. Strong, clear axioms help create confidence and trust.

An axiom is a starting point of reasoning. As classically conceived, an axiom is a premise so evident as to be accepted as true without controversy. An axiom is an unprovable rule or first principle accepted as true because it is self-evident or particularly useful. For example, one common axiom is the law of noncontradiction: "Contradictory statements cannot all be true in the same sense at the same time." Axioms are different from theorems, which require rigorous proof. The big bang theory or the theory of natural selection are both theorems.

As I describe a few more axioms that are useful for our study of philosophy and worldview, it is important to define a key term. *Perfection* is a challenging word to explain, but for our purposes here, I am using the word to mean what almost all of the dictionaries start with and what most people intuitively think of in regard to the concept. The word *perfection* used here is the state or quality of something or someone that cannot be improved upon; a condition of having no flaws. It is related to the ideas of *completeness*, *fullness*, and *wholeness*. Here are some more axioms:

> A perfect being must have perfect standards; therefore, one must be perfect in order to dwell with this perfect Being or to exist as this perfect Being.

> If an eternal state of perfection exists, then if one is not perfect, one must become perfect in order to exist in a state of perfection or to experience an eternal state of perfection.

> An imperfect being cannot become perfect perfectly if left to himself or herself, because one would need to be perfect in order to do this perfectly.

> If all that exists in the cosmos is matter and electricity expressed through pure cause-and-effect relationships, then existence for humanity is completely subject to cause and effect, and autonomous, independent freedom of choice (free will) cannot exist.

> If there is no spiritual realm or objective reality to the material world, then morality by necessity has to be internally subjective (relative) in a closed system of cause and effect.

If morality is internally subjective in a closed system, then the concepts of right and wrong, good and evil, fair and unfair, are essentially relative. All of morality is ultimately based on perceived personal preference or agreed upon by group consent.

If there is no actual distinction between a universal spirit and the human spirit, then there is no individual or autonomous human spirit; and consequently, there is no individual free will for humans.

Authentic grace is a completely free gift; therefore, the offering of this pure gift cannot be dependent on the receiver's attitude, behavior, motivation, perspective, understanding, ability, character, ethnicity, comprehension, intelligence, actions, etc., to receive this gift.

There are vast numbers of philosophical axioms. I chose to put a few here that I thought were useful to expose. They make for strong, healthy conversation, and they are trustworthy, tried, and true. All axioms are meant to be pondered and agreed with, and then they should be brought underground for your philosophical foundation. Let them settle in; they should feel rock-solid, firm, embedded, and comfortable. A natural response to an axiom would be, "Yes, of course—that's obvious" or "I never thought about it like that before, but that makes total sense."

If you do not understand one of these axioms or why it matters, start a conversation with your leader about the ones that do not click.

EXTEND YOUR LEARNING: Pick at least three of the axioms listed and find an image or create a visual aid, a cartoon, or a drawing to clarify and represent each message. Think along the lines of a meme, an Instagram post, or a magnet.

EXTEND YOUR LEARNING: Research some common axioms. (If you are researching online, do it in a group with a leader or parent—be careful, and use a healthy filter.) List three axioms from among the following: "philosophical axioms," "mathematical axioms," "humorous axioms," "faulty (false) axioms," or "religious axioms."

How and What to Trust: Subjective and Objective Truth

It is essential to understand that there are two functional and accepted types of truths. Speaker and teacher Mike Penninga states that various truths can end up in two different "truth buckets": *subjective* and *objective.**

Many people who approach philosophy and theology confuse this issue. Worse yet, many people have built a lifestyle from various philosophies and theologies, especially concerning morality, with a deep misunderstanding of this foundational approach to reality.

When building a house to live in, it is important to use the right materials at the right time in the right way. With weak axioms, we end up with a cracked, crumbling, leaky basement. When we confuse objective and subjective truths, it is like mixing mortar that is unsuitable for constructing a wall. The wall will look solid, but it will be weak and unsafe. When we lean on the wall or put any pressure on the wall, it will most likely come crashing down. Often the people who have made this mistake are blind or ignorant to this misappropriation of truth and

---

* Mike Penninga, "God, I Have a Question · Part 2 · Don't All Roads Lead to You?" Kelowna Gospel Fellowship Church, April 14, 2013, https://www.kgfchurch.com/2013/04/14/god-i-have-a-question-part-2-dont-all-paths-lead-to-you/.

what they are trusting, so they feel awkward at best and utterly foolish or defeated at worst when light is shed on the mistake.

Devastating personal and communal consequences can result from a simple lack of awareness or from intentional denial about the healthy practice of appropriate differentiation of the buckets into which we place truths. Furthermore, this responsibility has exponential impact on leaders! Teachers, parents, and mentors must clearly and continually articulate into which bucket they are putting the various lessons they teach.

Subjective truths are based purely on the perspective of the subject (person) making the decision; they are relative concepts based on personal preference, opinion, and perspective. These truths tell us more about the subject (the person and his or her feelings or opinions) than the object (the issue or item) in question.

Some subjective truths are:

+ Vanilla ice cream is the best flavor.
+ Your stained glass window is beautiful and inspiring.
+ Meat loaf is delicious.
+ It is a beautiful day outside.

Objective truths are true regardless of the perspective or feelings of the person making the decision or observation; they are universally trusted standards. These truths are focused entirely on the object in question rather than the subject (the person and his or her perspective, feelings, or opinions about the item or issue).

Some objective truths are:

+ There is a wide variety of ice cream flavors.
+ The stained glass window is broken.
+ This meat loaf is made of beef, onions, and ketchup.
+ It is sunny and seventy degrees outside with a gentle breeze.

As you work through the following learning adventures on this important topic, watch what happens when we consider the subjective and objective components of our daily lives with our family and friends and classmates. It is an interesting discussion to subjectively describe our favorite condiments, and it quickly becomes silly if we deem mustard to be morally evil as a choice for one's french fries. The conversation will carry a different weight and tone when we change out condiments for adultery, cheating, or gossip. The discussion ceases to be silly when we discuss whether anything is morally evil or not and, if something is, what is and what is not and why. You might find it interesting to research and discuss the differences between "ritual" and "ethical" morality in various religions, including your own, if you have one.

Hopefully you and your learning group or family will see the importance of navigating this terrain before we embark on this worldview adventure any further and what the implications are concerning the "philosophical house" metaphor for building and sustaining our worldviews. Remember that what we trust and what we have on our conscious and subconscious trust list affects every single decision we make and every interaction we have with others and with our environment.

LEARNING ADVENTURE

How and What to Trust: Personal Connections to Subjective/Objective Truth

For you personally:

1)

2)

For your family:

1)

2)

For your school:

1)

2)

For your culture:

1)

2)

Work in a small group to create two examples of *objective* truths . . .

Important for you personally:

1)

2)

Important for your family:

1)

2)

Important for your school:

1)

2)

Important for your culture:

1)

2)

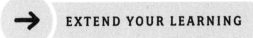

How and What to Trust: Discussion Starters

Create five distinct questions about subjective and objective truths (for example, what they are, examples of these, how to determine what is objective versus subjective). Use these questions to interview someone who is not part of your group, and write down his or her responses.

Question #1:

Response #1:

Question #2:

Response #2:

Question #3:

Response #3:

Question #4:

Response #4:

Question #5:

Response #5:

Below, write a short personal response to the discussion on subjective and objective truth. List at least three new insights you have about this topic that are essential to philosophy.

Four Perspectives on Morality

Morality is a challenging concept to explain because of the types, layers, implications, and functions of morality. Your attitude and perspective toward morality directly relate to how you define these terms and how you choose to interpret subjectivity versus objectivity. That choice in turn directly influences your daily behavior and decision making. What we are most concerned with here is where the authority and standards for these decisions come from. Do we simply get to decide what to do with our time and money and bodies? Does someone else decide? Or does an objective, absolute standard exist for everybody to follow?

IDEALISM

For a pure idealist, morality is objective based on the nature of the spiritual ideal as eternally good, beautiful, and true. Moral behaviors and decisions are defined as right and good based on the perfect ideal of what is good, beautiful, and true. However, morality feels subjective for idealists living on Faith Island based on each person's imperfect and incomplete personal interpretation of and limited access to the ideal, objective standards of what is perfectly good, perfectly beautiful, and perfectly true. It is intrinsically difficult for that which is imperfect, broken, and ugly to know and understand, let alone do and be, the perfectly good, beautiful, and true.

MATERIALISM

For an authentic materialist, morality is subjective at the core. It is internal and relative based completely on perspective and preference, like choosing an ice cream flavor. Because there is nothing objective outside of and distinct from the cause-and-effect nature of the material realm, morality appears to be based on self (on individual humans) or collectives of humans with no actual, real, objective authority or standards. However, morality feels objective when powerful people or organizations enforce individual or group preferences or when a community gives authority to a majority or a select group of people. We could even consider morality as part of a survival instinct, as many naturalists do, implying guidelines for ethical morality because acting ethically is in the best interest of the group that is trying to protect its gene pool. This feeling or appearance of objectivity can be subtly misleading for many materialists. Such moral standards are not actually objective; rather, they are the result of subjective majority preference, even if that is a preference for survival. If survival becomes morally "good" for our genes, what objective standard exists to say it is morally preferred to extinction? And which objective standard would a group use to decide which genes should survive over others if a choice were to be made?

MONISM

For a complete monist, morality is wholly subjective and is basically the same as that of a materialist. The difference is that the weight of one's preference often carries greater authority, because a monist can claim to be part of the universal being often called "god." In short, good and evil, right and wrong behavior and standards are based on the understanding of self as being part of the collective universe, which exists as god. The self is part of the universal, absolute authority of humanity's collective coexistence. However, morality for a monist, like that of a materialist, feels objective when moral "preference" is universally established, usually through human loyalty or majority rule. Moral standards can be objectified by tradition and rituals or by allegiance to a preferred aspect of behavior or a preferred standard. This often ends up manifesting itself in the form of allegiance to a "side" drawn from the dualistic and polarized nature of reality on earth, such as light and dark, birth and death, creation and decay, and so on.

THEISM

For a sincere theist, ethical morality for humans is objective based on the nature of the Creator God as the definer of and standard for morality. However, because God is a perfect, autonomous being separate from creation and from created beings, morality is actually subjective for God, who has the intrinsic power and authority to define morality. However, because perfection is that which cannot be improved upon and which has no flaw, even though God is a living being, God will never change moral standards. Interestingly for theists, morality often feels subjective in a similar way that perfection can feel subjective since it is based on one's personal interpretation of and limited access to God, God's nature, and God's revelation. This is how different religions and denominations within these religions can have a wide variety of moral standards, but all of them say they are based on God's perfect standards.

Four Perspectives on Morality: Ethical Dilemmas

Describe how a real person from each of the four worldviews would navigate various ethical dilemmas. The key to this is to not place judgment upon the decision—it is to help reveal what each person is *basing* the decision on. What does each person *use* in order to make the choices he or she is faced with for the following situations?

WHETHER OR NOT TO LIE:

+ Pure idealist response:

+ Authentic materialist response:

+ Complete monist response:

+ Religious theist response:

WHETHER OR NOT TO CHEAT ON A TEST:

+ Pure idealist response:

+ Authentic materialist response:

+ Complete monist response:

+ Religious theist response:

WHETHER OR NOT TO STEAL A LARGE AMOUNT OF MONEY:

+ Pure idealist response:

+ Authentic materialist response:

+ Complete monist response:

+ Religious theist response:

**WHETHER OR NOT TO HELP THOSE WHO ARE
LESS FORTUNATE THAN YOU:**

+ Pure idealist response:

+ Authentic materialist response:

+ Complete monist response:

+ Religious theist response:

EXTEND YOUR LEARNING: Create and discuss real-life scenarios that pertain to your immediate community, or pick some scenes from your favorite books or movies. How do people's choices reveal their worldview?

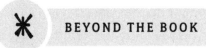

Four Perspectives on Perfection

Your attitude and perspective toward perfection directly relate to how you behave and make decisions all the time. Is perfection subjective or objective? After death, are we able to become one with perfection or dwell with a perfect God?

IDEALISM

For pure idealists, perfection and wholeness comprise an objective, ideal state of being, based on the nature of the "spiritual ideal." This is because idealists trust that only the ideal spiritual realm is really real. For idealists, the material world is broken; it is not ideal and can always be improved upon. If we want to exist forever, we must strive until we actually become that one, perfect ideal that is spiritual, not physical. Perfection is that which is eternally good, beautiful, and true. There is only one "form" of perfection. It is eternal because it is perfect and will last forever in that state. It has no flaw; it is the only standard by which all things are measured. For idealists, perfection is objective; it exists as true and perfect whether humans like it or know it.

MATERIALISM

For an authentic materialist, perfection and wholeness are literally in the eye of the beholder, and therefore they are utterly and completely relative and subjective. Because there is no outside, objective standard for perfection, and because everybody has their own unique, individual, personal perspective on the world from within the world, materialists have no authoritative, purely objective standard for making verifiable comparisons. People can agree on standards, or they can pretend that there is objectivity, but this is fabricated and malleable.

MONISM

For a complete monist, perfection and wholeness are part of existence; therefore, everything is perfect as it exists. This is similar to the materialist perspective on perfection; it simply adds in the weight of spirituality. Monists will concede that there is nothing objective, above, beyond, or separate from the universal collective coexistence of everything. Consequently, the concept of perfection is always subjective because there is nothing that is distinct from the unified existence of the universe. As such, monists do not believe in an all-powerful creator God in the sense that theists do, so there is no basis for any objective comparison or standard. Often a monist will refer to existence with authoritative vocabulary like "god" or "the unifying life force." A monist believes everything in existence to be a part of god, who in nature fits the definition of perfection as that which cannot be improved upon. Therefore, everything is perfect as it is, if only we had the eyes and willingness to see it as such. Everything that exists is perfect simply because it exists.

THEISM

For a religious theist, perfection and wholeness exist as defined by an objective, perfect, living being. This being is perfect, eternal, and complete and cannot be improved upon. This being is also distinct and independent from creation and from created beings. In theism, this being is usually referred to as God. God as the perfect Creator has the objectivity and authority to decide or declare what is perfect. Thus, humanity is subject to God's definition of and standards for perfection. This is a great place to see an axiom come into play: because God is perfect, God will have perfect standards; therefore, one would have to be perfect to dwell with this perfect being. Another interesting point on perfection for theists surfaces when created human beings reject or differ on their interpretation of or relationship with God, the perfect standard of perfection.

Four Perspectives on Perfection: What Is Perfect?

Describe in a few sentences how you would need to paint a picture, play a song, and compete as an athlete based on how each worldview defines perfection.

IDEALISM

Artistic/poetic approach to perfection:

Musical approach to perfection:

Athletic approach to perfection:

MATERIALISM

Artistic/poetic approach to perfection:

Musical approach to perfection:

Athletic approach to perfection:

MONISM

Artistic/poetic approach to perfection:

Musical approach to perfection:

Athletic approach to perfection:

THEISM

Artistic/poetic approach to perfection:

Musical approach to perfection:

Athletic approach to perfection:

Reflections on Morality and Perfection

While there is some overlap between these different worldviews, there are also differences that are polar opposites. For example, theism is similar to idealism, but instead of a state of existence or an abstract concept, "form," or idea, the perfect ideal is a being who is alive, interacts with creation and created beings, and has authority over these other beings. Thus, there is the potential for unlimited, independent definitions of perfection and wholeness as defined by this objective, perfect authority. Theism is also different from monism: in theism, God is separate from creation the way an artist is separate from his or her painting. In monism, everything is god; the painting is god, and god is the painting.

These definitions shape not only our perception and understanding of reality but also how we relate to one another on a daily basis. When we fail to understand that different people in a single conversation may be utilizing the same word to describe separate perspectives with vastly different consequences, we delve into a world of misunderstanding based on false assumptions.

Imagine four people having a cup of coffee and discussing perfection. An authentic materialist and a complete monist would get along pretty well as they discuss their differences and similarities about what is perfect. There is no heaven or hell or objective standard, just undiluted freedom to describe perfection based on whatever standard is preferred.

The pure idealist and the sincere theist could debate the standards and sources they trust to define what is perfect. A theist might discuss access to this standard through a personal relationship with this living being called God. An idealist will most likely describe this standard as a state of being. While a theist spends time with God in a relationship, the state of perfect existence that an idealist calls god is not a being that an idealist could spend time with. An idealist strives to become one with this ideal. An idealist would need to become god and become perfect in order to exist as god. For the theist, because this perfect God has perfect standards, the theist would need to become perfect according to God's standards in order to dwell with this God. However, a theist never becomes God. This conversation between a theist and an idealist would naturally turn into a discussion on the methodology for attaining and sustaining this state of perfection.

EXTEND YOUR LEARNING: In a small group, practice having discussions on morality and perfection while each is pretending to be someone who subscribes to one of the four worldviews. Use the examples from the previous activity on art, music, and athletics. Consider using the scenarios from the lessons on morality to practice these worldview dialogues. You can extend your learning further by having discussions with people who represent these various worldviews. Be kind and considerate in your conversations. Take notes on what you are learning. Come to your teacher, parents, or mentor with questions and comments.

Philosophy and the Four Views of Reality

In your hearts revere Christ as Lord. Always be prepared to give an answer to everyone who asks you to give the reason for the hope that you have. But do this with gentleness and respect.

1 PETER 3:15, NIV

Outline

These questions are essential to our learning and growth for this course of study. They are the focus of part 2 of the *Inklings on Philosophy and Worldview* book and the driving force behind this guidebook. The book, your instruction, the supplemental podcasts (available at IntheTrueMyth.org), and the assignments in this guidebook are all developed to help you answer these questions:

1. What are the four dominant worldviews, and what is on their different trust lists?
2. What are the seven basic questions of reality?
3. What does a pure idealist trust?
4. What does an authentic materialist trust?
5. What does a complete monist trust?
6. What does a religious theist trust?
7. How can I treat all worldviews with dignity, honor, and respect? How can I be loving to all people on this worldview adventure?

PART TWO SUGGESTED READINGS

○ All of part 2 from the *Inklings on Philosophy and Worldview* book (pages 51–111)
○ Philippians (pages 144–152)
○ John Keats: "When I Have Fears That I May Cease to Be" (page 161)
○ Friedrich Nietzsche: "The Madman" (pages 163–165)
○ Ecclesiastes 1–3, 12 (pages 168–174)
○ Andy Weir: "The Egg" (supplemental)
○ 1 John (pages 185–194)
○ Mason Jennings: "I Love You and Buddha Too" (supplemental)
○ The Gospel of John (supplemental)

PART TWO LEARNING OPPORTUNITIES
Learning Adventures

○ "Open Our Eyes So We Can See!" (pages 108–110)
○ The Lord's Prayer, Our Prayer, a Kingdom Prayer (pages 115–117)
○ The Four Trust Lists Pre/Post Assessment (pages 122–128)
○ The Four Trust Lists Pre/Post Assessment (Continued) (pages 129–130)
○ The Philosophical Trust List of a Pure Idealist (pages 136–137)
○ The Philosophical Trust List of an Authentic Materialist (pages 155–156)
○ John Keats and Materialism (pages 161–162)
○ Nietzsche's "Madman" and Me (pages 166–167)
○ The Philosophical Trust List of a Complete Monist (pages 177–178)
○ The Philosophical Trust List of a Religious Theist (pages 197–198)
○ "The Inch" (pages 206–208)

Extend Your Learning

○ Reality Check for Idealism (pages 138–141)
○ Words of the Buddha (pages 142–143)
○ Reality Check for Materialism (pages 157–160)

O Reality Check for Monism (pages 179–182)
O Monism and "The Egg" (pages 183–184)
O Reality Check for Religious Theism (pages 199–202)
O A Discussion of "I Love You and Buddha Too" (pages 203–205)
O The Big Questions: An Interview (pages 211–212)
O The Big Questions: Another Interview (pages 213–214)
O Part Two Projects (pages 215–216)

Exploring Ideas

O A Kingdom Mind-Set and 1 Corinthians 12–13 (pages 118–121)
O Philippians and Idealism (pages 144–152)
O "The Madman" by Friedrich Nietzsche (pages 163–165)
O Ecclesiastes and Materialism (pages 168–174)
O 1 John and Monism (pages 185–194)
O The Gospel of John and Theism (page 209–210)

Beyond the Book

O Kingdom Community and Worldview (pages 111–114)
O The Trust Lists: The Four Worldviews at a Glance
   (pages 131–133)
O Idealism (pages 134–135)
O Materialism (pages 153–154)
O Monism (pages 175–176)
O Theism (pages 195–196)

Coordinates and Bearings for Learning Adventures: Part Two

Part 2 is meant to guide you to the destination of awareness of and information about the seven big questions of philosophy and how the four main worldviews—idealism, materialism, monism, and theism—answer these big questions. This section is imbued with tough questions, sticky concepts, and dense reading. This will be the first time we test the gear acquired in part 1. It is very easy to get tripped up and caught in the difficulty of these concepts, but if we use our gear properly, it will protect us and help us to get farther on the journey. This part has some great nuggets of truth if we keep our eyes and minds open.

This section of your learning journey will focus on and invite you into . . .

Understanding philosophy as a means to an end and
    not an end in itself.
Viewing philosophy as a powerful tool to build your
    worldview.

Remembering and embracing love as an essential ingredient in your worldview.

Examining the seven big worldview questions and the four main worldviews.

PART 2 SUMMARY

In part 2, we will look at the four main worldviews in which humans place their trust and how each worldview answers some of life's essential questions. Idealism, materialism, monism, and theism each hold a portion of the truth, and each provides its followers with answers that influence how they live. In this part, we are not exalting any one of these worldviews above the others, nor are we setting them up only to knock them down. We will look at each one with as unbiased a view as possible.

"Open Our Eyes So We Can See!"

Read 2 Kings 6:8-23, the story of Elisha and the angel army, and answer the questions that follow.

⁸When the king of Aram was at war with Israel, he would confer with his officers and say, "We will mobilize our forces at such and such a place."

⁹But immediately Elisha, the man of God, would warn the king of Israel, "Do not go near that place, for the Arameans are planning to mobilize their troops there." ¹⁰So the king of Israel would send word to the place indicated by the man of God. Time and again Elisha warned the king, so that he would be on the alert there.

¹¹The king of Aram became very upset over this. He called his officers together and demanded, "Which of you is the traitor? Who has been informing the king of Israel of my plans?"

¹²"It's not us, my lord the king," one of the officers replied. "Elisha, the prophet in Israel, tells the king of Israel even the words you speak in the privacy of your bedroom!"

¹³"Go and find out where he is," the king commanded, "so I can send troops to seize him."

And the report came back: "Elisha is at Dothan." ¹⁴So one night the king of Aram sent a great army with many chariots and horses to surround the city.

¹⁵When the servant of the man of God got up early the next morning and went outside, there were troops, horses, and chariots everywhere. "Oh, sir, what will we do now?" the young man cried to Elisha.

¹⁶"Don't be afraid!" Elisha told him. "For there are more on our side than on theirs!" ¹⁷Then Elisha prayed, "O LORD, open his eyes and let him see!" The LORD opened the young man's eyes, and when he looked up, he saw that the hillside around Elisha was filled with horses and chariots of fire.

¹⁸As the Aramean army advanced toward him, Elisha prayed, "O LORD, please make them blind." So the LORD struck them with blindness as Elisha had asked.

¹⁹Then Elisha went out and told them, "You have come the wrong way! This isn't the right city! Follow me, and I will take you to the man you are looking for." And he led them to the city of Samaria.

²⁰As soon as they had entered Samaria, Elisha prayed, "O LORD, now open their eyes and let them see." So the LORD opened their eyes, and they discovered that they were in the middle of Samaria.

²¹When the king of Israel saw them, he shouted to Elisha, "My father, should I kill them? Should I kill them?"

²²"Of course not!" Elisha replied. "Do we kill prisoners of war? Give them food and drink and send them home again to their master."

²³So the king made a great feast for them and then sent them home to their master. After that, the Aramean raiders stayed away from the land of Israel.

Answer these questions:

1. List and describe as many aspects of Prime Reality as you can find in this story. How did these aspects differ from the perceptions of the characters in the story?

2. How did the emotional state of Elisha's servant change throughout the story?

3. How might your already-open eyes need to be opened right now?

4. Write a paragraph about what you think it would be like to be Elisha's servant in the story. How would you have reacted?

5. Rewrite verses 15-17 in a modern local setting for you and your friends:

Kingdom Community and Worldview

How will you help to create a learning environment that is saturated with love and honor for all people?*

The *Inklings on Philosophy and Worldview* book and this corresponding guidebook are designed to help you on your life's journey. Ultimately, this philosophy and worldview adventure should point you to a deeper connection and relationship with Christ! When we know and respond to Christ's love and gracious gift of salvation, when we understand that we are beloved children of God, and when we have a worldview that allows for the Bible to come alive and be active in our daily lives, we are ready for the call to discipleship. In this book and guidebook, you are learning what it means to have an authentic Christ-centered biblical worldview, and this is what makes a lifetime of discipleship sustainable. Discipleship is intended to be learned in fellowship, thus it is essential to create a Kingdom community. Otherwise, discipleship will not last, will self-destruct, or will become destructive to others, particularly to those

---

* If you are in a church, classroom, family, or small-group setting, be sure to check out the resources available on building and sustaining a Kingdom community of love and honor at InTheTrueMyth.org, "Kingdom Community."

you are trying to serve. **To sum up: a Christ-centered, biblical world-view makes authentic biblical discipleship possible, and the Kingdom community makes it applicable, and both the worldview and the community make discipleship sustainable—something that will last.**

I focus on seven core Kingdom community values:

+ love
+ safety
+ respect
+ honor
+ community
+ learning
+ joy

Community, particularly an educational community, thrives within a healthy structure and safe boundaries, and God provides life-giving guidelines for both.* G. K. Chesterton writes in *Orthodoxy*:

Doctrine and discipline may be walls; but they are the walls of a playground. Christianity is the only frame which has preserved the [appropriate] pleasure of Paganism. We might fancy some children playing on the flat grassy top of some tall island in the sea. So long as there was a wall round the cliff's edge they could fling themselves into every frantic game and make the place the noisiest of nurseries. But the walls were knocked down, leaving the naked peril of the precipice. They did not fall over; but when their friends returned to them they were all huddled in terror in the center of the island; and their song had ceased.

---

* The material in this and the following paragraph is adapted from the teaching on Kingdom community on IntheTrueMyth.org.

Likewise, in his famous poem "Mending Wall," Robert Frost subtly but confidently describes our innate need for healthy boundaries, penning, "Good fences make good neighbors."

Building a safe and vivacious culture in our schools, churches, and homes must be a top priority! Jesus says in Luke 12:31, "Seek the Kingdom of God above all else," and in John 13:35, he says, "Your love for one another will prove to the world that you are my disciples." These two teachings are at the core of Jesus' pedagogy. Furthermore, Jesus gave children the place of highest honor when he said, "Let the children come to me. Don't stop them!" (Matthew 19:14) and made their worldview a foundation of his Kingdom worldview. Additionally, he made the safety of each child of utmost priority (see Matthew 18:6). The Kingdom community material on IntheTrueMyth.org is designed to help you learn how to develop, integrate, and sustain a Kingdom community model in your family, school, church, and classroom.

How can I contribute to being more loving on this worldview journey?

Love is Jesus' command to his disciples, and Paul describes love as "a way of life that is best of all" (1 Corinthians 12:31). Love is the "way of life that is best" for everybody to grow in adventures in learning, particularly in conversations about philosophy and worldview.

In 1 Corinthians 13:4-7, Paul gives several attributes of love, which I've listed below. Ask this about each of the attributes: *Am I?* Prayerfully write out "God is . . ." and "I am . . ." next to each of the following, and consider what that attribute will look like in your life. Be alert to how the Holy Spirit guides your responses and direction for this course of study.

LOVE IS . . .
+ Patient
+ Kind
+ Not jealous
+ Not boastful
+ Not proud

+ Not dishonoring to others ("not . . . rude!")
+ Not self-seeking ("does not demand its own way")
+ Not easily angered ("not irritable")
+ Forgiving ("it keeps no record of being wronged")
+ Pure ("does not rejoice about injustice")
+ Truthful ("rejoices whenever the truth wins out")
+ Trusting ("never loses faith")
+ Hopeful
+ Persevering ("never gives up" and "endures through every circumstance")

FOR DISCUSSION

1. Why is each aspect of love important for a learning environment?

2. What would this kind of love look like in your class, friendships, home, business, road trip, and so on? What would it look like in your interactions with others who have different values, beliefs, and worldviews?

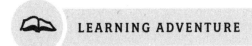
The Lord's Prayer, Our Prayer, a Kingdom Prayer

"May your Kingdom come soon": this is our goal, vision, and mission. It is a prayer for authentic discipleship.

Use the space provided to describe how each section of the Lord's Prayer invites a discussion on worldview. Discuss your answers in a small group.

MATTHEW 6:9-13

Our Father in heaven, may your name be kept holy.

May your Kingdom come soon. May your will be done on earth, as it is in heaven.

Give us today the food we need.

And forgive us our sins, as we have forgiven those who sin against us.

And don't let us yield to temptation.

But rescue us from the evil one.

Additional questions for reflection and discussion:

1. What are the implications of Jesus calling God "Father" and then teaching us to call God "Father"?

2. What does it mean to have God's will be done on earth (here and now) as it is in heaven?

3. Who is "the evil one," and what is the standard used for calling him evil? What makes "the evil one" evil?

A Kingdom Mind-Set and 1 Corinthians 12–13

ANALYZING THE TEXT

As you read this selection from Paul's first letter to the Corinthians, ask questions such as, "What are the connections to how to approach the study of philosophy and worldview with dignity and respect? How can I engage with people whose views are different from mine in a loving, honoring, and respectful way?"

Highlight or underline at least three verses or passages in these chapters from 1 Corinthians that you find engaging, and be prepared to explain why you picked those verses.

SPACE TO WRITE OR DOODLE

1 CORINTHIANS 12–13

Chapter 12

Now, dear brothers and sisters, regarding your question about the special abilities the Spirit gives us. I don't want you to misunderstand this. ²You know that when you were still pagans, you were led astray and swept along in worshiping speechless idols. ³So I want you to know that no one speaking by the Spirit of God will curse Jesus, and no one can say Jesus is Lord, except by the Holy Spirit.

[4]There are different kinds of spiritual gifts, but the same Spirit is the source of them all. [5]There are different kinds of service, but we serve the same Lord. [6]God works in different ways, but it is the same God who does the work in all of us.

[7]A spiritual gift is given to each of us so we can help each other. [8]To one person the Spirit gives the ability to give wise advice; to another the same Spirit gives a message of special knowledge. [9]The same Spirit gives great faith to another, and to someone else the one Spirit gives the gift of healing. [10]He gives one person the power to perform miracles, and another the ability to prophesy. He gives someone else the ability to discern whether a message is from the Spirit of God or from another spirit. Still another person is given the ability to speak in unknown languages, while another is given the ability to interpret what is being said. [11]It is the one and only Spirit who distributes all these gifts. He alone decides which gift each person should have.

[12]The human body has many parts, but the many parts make up one whole body. So it is with the body of Christ. [13]Some of us are Jews, some are Gentiles, some are slaves, and some are free. But we have all been baptized into one body by one Spirit, and we all share the same Spirit.

[14]Yes, the body has many different parts, not just one part. [15]If the foot says, "I am not a part of the body because I am not a hand," that does not make it any less a part of the body. [16]And if the ear says, "I am not part of the body because I am not an eye," would that make it any less a part of the body? [17]If the whole body were an eye, how would you hear? Or if your whole body were an ear, how would you smell anything?

[18]But our bodies have many parts, and God has put each part just where he wants it. [19]How strange a body would

be if it had only one part! [20]Yes, there are many parts, but only one body. [21]The eye can never say to the hand, "I don't need you." The head can't say to the feet, "I don't need you."

[22]In fact, some parts of the body that seem weakest and least important are actually the most necessary. [23]And the parts we regard as less honorable are those we clothe with the greatest care. So we carefully protect those parts that should not be seen, [24]while the more honorable parts do not require this special care. So God has put the body together such that extra honor and care are given to those parts that have less dignity. [25]This makes for harmony among the members, so that all the members care for each other. [26]If one part suffers, all the parts suffer with it, and if one part is honored, all the parts are glad.

[27]All of you together are Christ's body, and each of you is a part of it. [28]Here are some of the parts God has appointed for the church:

first are apostles,
second are prophets,
third are teachers,
then those who do miracles,
those who have the gift of healing,
those who can help others,
those who have the gift of leadership,
those who speak in unknown languages.

[29]Are we all apostles? Are we all prophets? Are we all teachers? Do we all have the power to do miracles? [30]Do we all have the gift of healing? Do we all have the ability to speak in unknown languages? Do we all have the ability to interpret unknown languages? Of course not! [31]So you should earnestly desire the most helpful gifts.

But now let me show you a way of life that is best of all.

Chapter 13

If I could speak all the languages of earth and of angels, but didn't love others, I would only be a noisy gong or a clanging cymbal. [2]If I had the gift of prophecy, and if I understood all of God's secret plans and possessed all knowledge, and if I had such faith that I could move mountains, but didn't love others, I would be nothing. [3]If I gave everything I have to the poor and even sacrificed my body, I could boast about it; but if I didn't love others, I would have gained nothing.

[4]Love is patient and kind. Love is not jealous or boastful or proud [5]or rude. It does not demand its own way. It is not irritable, and it keeps no record of being wronged. [6]It does not rejoice about injustice but rejoices whenever the truth wins out. [7]Love never gives up, never loses faith, is always hopeful, and endures through every circumstance.

[8]Prophecy and speaking in unknown languages and special knowledge will become useless. But love will last forever! [9]Now our knowledge is partial and incomplete, and even the gift of prophecy reveals only part of the whole picture! [10]But when the time of perfection comes, these partial things will become useless.

[11]When I was a child, I spoke and thought and reasoned as a child. But when I grew up, I put away childish things. [12]Now we see things imperfectly, like puzzling reflections in a mirror, but then we will see everything with perfect clarity. All that I know now is partial and incomplete, but then I will know everything completely, just as God now knows me completely.

[13]Three things will last forever—faith, hope, and love—and the greatest of these is love.

The Four Trust Lists Pre/Post Assessment

Use a red pen to fill in the blanks before you study the four worldviews. Try it again with a green pen at the end of your study of part 2 and then again with a blue pen at the end of part 3.

PURE IDEALISM

1. What is the nature of reality? What is really real?

2. Who is God? What is God?

3. What is a human being? What is humankind?

4. What is the basis of and standard for morality? How do I decide between right and wrong, and who or what is the basis of moral authority?

5. What happens to humans at death?

6. What is the meaning and purpose of human history? What is the essence of human interaction and relationships?

7. Why are we here? Where are we going? What is the purpose of human existence?

Offer some specific "Good News" from Jesus to a pure idealist:

AUTHENTIC MATERIALISM

1. What is the nature of reality? What is really real?

2. Who is God? What is God?

3. What is a human being? What is humankind?

4. What is the basis of and standard for morality? How do I decide between right and wrong, and who or what is the basis of moral authority?

5. What happens to humans at death?

6. What is the meaning and purpose of human history? What is the essence of human interaction and relationships?

7. Why are we here? Where are we going? What is the purpose of human existence?

Offer some specific "Good News" from Jesus to an authentic materialist:

COMPLETE MONISM

1. What is the nature of reality? What is really real?

2. Who is God? What is God?

3. What is a human being? What is humankind?

4. What is the basis of and standard for morality? How do I decide between right and wrong, and who or what is the basis of moral authority?

5. What happens to humans at death?

6. What is the meaning and purpose of human history? What is the essence of human interaction and relationships?

7. Why are we here? Where are we going? What is the purpose of human existence?

Offer some specific "Good News" from Jesus to a complete monist:

RELIGIOUS THEISM

1. What is the nature of reality? What is really real?

2. Who is God? What is God?

3. What is a human being? What is humankind?

4. What is the basis of and standard for morality? How do I decide between right and wrong, and who or what is the basis of moral authority?

5. What happens to humans at death?

6. What is the meaning and purpose of human history? What is the essence of human interaction and relationships?

7. Why are we here? Where are we going? What is the purpose of human existence?

Offer some specific "Good News" from Jesus to a religious theist:

The Four Trust Lists Pre/Post Assessment (Continued)

Use a red pen to fill this out as well as you can before you study the four worldviews. Try it again with a green pen at the end of your study of part 2 and then again with a blue pen at the end of part 3.

In the space provided, pretend that you are responding to the following questions: "I have heard you are studying philosophy and worldview. Could you help me understand the four different beliefs in a few brief sentences? What are some practical examples of people who believe each view? And what do these people basically believe?"

PURE IDEALISTS

_____

_____

_____

_____

_____

_____

AUTHENTIC MATERIALISTS

_____

_____

_____

_____

_____

_____

_____

COMPLETE MONISTS

_____

_____

_____

_____

_____

_____

_____

RELIGIOUS THEISTS

_____

_____

_____

_____

_____

_____

_____

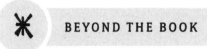

The Trust Lists:
The Four Worldviews
at a Glance

You may not live what you profess; but you live what you believe,
what you trust. It is inescapable!

DR. WILLIAM E. BROWN

The following grid provides another practical way to organize the basic information from part 2 of the *Inklings on Philosophy and Worldview* book, especially chapters 6 and 7. This tool offers an efficient way to compare and contrast the four basic answers to the seven big questions presented in the book. Every individual will, by necessity, find himself or herself somewhere on the trust lists grid when answering life's essential questions. I suggest that you highlight the answers you lean toward as you look at the grid.

Furthermore, the grid can be helpful when having a conversation with someone about the various differences in worldviews. This grid, combined with the essential truths of "Faith Island," invites everyone into dialogue concerning the consequences of their own choices in relation to what they are trusting. Often the consequences for trusting various options are astronomically different. That difference is worthy of a closer look.

Views of Reality & Core Philosophy Questions	Pure Idealism	Authentic Materialism	Complete Monism	Religious Theism
1. What is the nature of reality? What is really real?	*Only* the spiritual is really real, and reality is a state of eternal spiritual perfection.	*Only* the material (the natural) is really real; there is no spiritual realm.	The spiritual and the material are *both* really real, existing as one entity. Reality presents itself as dual in nature, yet all of existence is ultimately one interconnected unity.	The spiritual and the material are *both* real yet independent, interdependent, and intradependent with each other.
2. Who or what is God?	The impersonal, eternal, perfect spiritual ideal is what people often call "god." It is absolute, complete truth, beauty, and goodness.	There is no objective powerful being outside of the material. God is a figment of human creativity and imagination, a creative idea or concept.	Everything is "god." Everything and everybody in the universe are an integral, interconnected part of the unity of life called "god."	There is a distinct God that is the all-powerful Creator, sustainer, and giver of all of life. God is personal and has personality.
3. What is a human being? What is humankind? (Who am I? What am I?)	Humans exist as one of the infinite, incomplete, imperfect replicas or "shadows" of the real (eternal) ideal state of spiritual perfection.	Human beings are fascinating, unique, and highly complex systems of matter and electricity that are beautifully aware of "self" and "others."	Humans are unique, unrepeatable parts of "god"; they are part of the one body of the universe and the entirety of reality referred to as "god."	Humans are a distinct, wonderful creation made in the image of God but not possessing the exact nature of God or existing as an extension or part of God.
4. What is the basis of and standard for morality? How do I decide between right and wrong, and who or what is the basis for moral authority?	All morality is objective and based on the nature of the impersonal perfect spiritual ideal, which is absolute truth, perfect beauty, and complete goodness.	All morality is ultimately subjective and based exclusively or collectively on self, majority, and power.	Morality is completely subjective, based on one's individual preference as a part of the interconnected universal reality called "god," and thus morality is relative.	All ethical morality is objective based on the personal, all-powerful nature of God, who is perfect and good. God (and God's word and nature) is the standard for and author of morality.

Views of Reality & Core Philosophy Questions	Pure Idealism	Authentic Materialism	Complete Monism	Religious Theism
5. What happens to humans at death?	When we die, perfection is attained and we become one with the state of spiritual perfection and/or we cease to exist as images of perfection and as imperfect "selves."	Humans cease to be aware of their existence at the point of death.	When we die, we "morph" into another part of existence and another component of the universal reality, which is "god."	When we die, we obtain individual perfection and exist eternally in continual relationship with the perfect personal God, or we remain in an imperfect, incomplete state and necessarily exist separated from God.
6. What is the meaning and purpose of human history? What is the essence of human interaction and relationships?	History and human memory are records of humans striving to escape nonexistence and attain an ideal state of spiritual perfection.	"History is a linear stream of events linked by cause and effect"* in a closed system (such as natural selection). Human interaction is literally chemistry and pure cause and effect.	History and human memory consist of the repository of collective memories of our collective coexistence as "god."	History is a "linear, meaningful sequence of events leading to the fulfillment of God's purposes for humanity" in an open system.** History is the true, epic adventure story of God's interaction with humankind.
7. Why are we here? Where are we going? What is the purpose of human existence?	We exist only to achieve and sustain an ideal state of spiritual perfection.	Humans get to create their own individual and collective meaning for life.	Every human has the exciting opportunity to continue experiencing being various components of universal reality—of "god"—forever.	At least one reason that humans exist is to enjoy and experience a meaningful relationship with the Creator and Sustainer of life.

---

* James Sire, *The Universe Next Door* (Downers Grove, IL: InterVarsity Press, 2009), 80.
** James Sire, *The Universe Next Door* (Downer's Grove, IL: InterVarsity Press, 2009), 22–23.

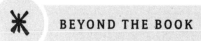

BEYOND THE BOOK

Idealism

Idealism: We are striving to exist as spiritual perfection, the spiritual ideal (as "god" or as part of "god").

Pure idealists trust that only the spiritual is the eternal fabric of Prime Reality. True idealists have a foundational understanding that the non-material "perfected idea" is eternal, beautiful, true, and good. It has a weight and realness to it that cannot be replicated or materialized. This understanding leads idealists to a greater awareness that the ideal exists fully in a spiritual reality and is merely (often poorly) represented in the physical. For all of the physical world, but particularly for humans, objects are essentially "imperfect shadows" or "incomplete imitations" of the spiritual ideal and are trying to become one with ultimate reality. This is an enlightened state of spiritual perfection. Currently, humans exist on earth only as the various, unlimited imperfect "images" of perfection. They retain the potential for eternal existence in a state of perfection in the real ideal, perfect spiritual realm. Humans are personally responsible for making themselves into the ideal, for becoming perfectly good, beautiful, and true in order to exist fully and eternally as spiritual perfection, escaping nonexistence as incomplete shadowy replicas.

Some religions, isms, and ways that construct their trust lists from this philosophy:

+ Buddhism
+ Much of Hinduism
+ Taoism
+ _____
+ _____
+ _____

EXTEND YOUR LEARNING: Find or draw some images to ponder and discuss that relate to this description of idealism.

The Philosophical Trust List of a Pure Idealist

Fill in the chart with some of the major cultural, religious, social, and personal consequences of adopting the pure idealist's trust list.

Big Questions of life	Pure Idealism	Some Major Cultural, Religious, Social, and Personal Consequences of This Trust List
1. What is the nature of reality? What is really real?	Only the spiritual is really real and reality is a state of eternal spiritual perfection.	
2. Who or what is God?	The impersonal, eternal, perfect spiritual ideal is what people often call "god." It is absolute, complete truth, beauty, and goodness.	

Big Questions of life	Pure Idealism	Some Major Cultural, Religious, Social, and Personal Consequences of This Trust List
3. What is a human being? What is humankind? (Who am I? What am I?)	Humans exist as one of the infinite, incomplete, imperfect replicas or "shadows" of the real (eternal) ideal state of spiritual perfection.	
4. What is the basis of and standard for morality? How do I decide between right and wrong, and who or what is the basis for moral authority?	All morality is objective and based on the nature of the impersonal perfect spiritual ideal, which is absolute truth, perfect beauty, and complete goodness.	
5. What happens to humans at death?	When we die, perfection is attained and we become one with the state of spiritual perfection and/or we cease to exist as images of perfection and as imperfect "selves."	
6. What is the meaning and purpose of human history? What is the essence of human interaction and relationships?	History and human memory are records of humans striving to escape nonexistence and attain an ideal state of spiritual perfection.	
7. Why are we here? Where are we going? What is the purpose of human existence?	We exist only to achieve and sustain an ideal state of spiritual perfection.	

Reality Check for Idealism

Take time to do some (safe) research to see how idealism has influenced the categories below. A good library is best for this, but the Internet, with a good filter, will also be helpful. This critical personal research and discovery will create a firm foundation for discussion when you realize that real people believe these things and live their daily lives based on the answers this philosophy provides. Consider doing a "show and tell" from your research on this worldview.

CULTURAL CONNECTIONS:

_____

_____

_____

_____

_____

_____

_____

POETRY AND BOOKS:

_____

_____

_____

_____

_____

_____

_____

ART/ARTISTS:

_____

_____

_____

_____

_____

_____

_____

FILM:

_____

_____

_____

_____

_____

_____

_____

MUSIC:

_____

_____

_____

_____

_____

_____

_____

RELIGIONS:

_____

_____

_____

_____

_____

_____

_____

SACRED/CORE TEXTS:

_____

_____

_____

_____

_____

_____

_____

HISTORICAL FIGURES:

_____

_____

_____

_____

_____

_____

_____

INFLUENTIAL/FAMOUS PEOPLE:

_____

_____

_____

_____

_____

_____

_____

KEY LANDMARKS/HISTORICAL SIGNIFICANCE:

_____

_____

_____

_____

_____

_____

_____

Words of the Buddha

1. Research, read, and ponder some of the common words of the Buddha. Record these on the next page.
2. Write a general response to the popular Buddhist truths, quotes, and proverbs you encountered.
3. Locate and write out Bible verses and their references next to the Buddhist quotes that support, are similar to, or are antithetical to these words of the Buddha. What did you observe during this exercise?
4. Which of these quotes would you tweet or post on social media? Why? Which ones would you not tweet or post on your social media? Why?
5. What are three or four new insights about idealism that you have after completing this exercise?

SPACE FOR NOTES ON WORDS OF THE BUDDHA

Philippians and Idealism

ANALYZING THE TEXT

Read and annotate the apostle Paul's letter to the church at Philippi in one sitting. Pretend you are a member of that church. Where do you see connections to the discussion on idealism and the religions, ways, and isms that base their trust lists on this philosophical approach to reality? The connections you make can be subtle, overt, literary, historical, artistic, personal, or metaphoric. How does Philippians 3:8 speak to an idealist or a "Christian idealist" in a unique and profound way?

Underline at least three verses that you find engaging, and be prepared to explain why you picked those verses.

PHILIPPIANS

Chapter 1

This letter is from Paul and Timothy, slaves of Christ Jesus.

I am writing to all of God's holy people in Philippi who belong to Christ Jesus, including the church leaders and deacons.

[2]May God our Father and the Lord Jesus Christ give you grace and peace.

³Every time I think of you, I give thanks to my God. ⁴Whenever I pray, I make my requests for all of you with joy, ⁵for you have been my partners in spreading the Good News about Christ from the time you first heard it until now. ⁶And I am certain that God, who began the good work within you, will continue his work until it is finally finished on the day when Christ Jesus returns.

⁷So it is right that I should feel as I do about all of you, for you have a special place in my heart. You share with me the special favor of God, both in my imprisonment and in defending and confirming the truth of the Good News. ⁸God knows how much I love you and long for you with the tender compassion of Christ Jesus.

⁹I pray that your love will overflow more and more, and that you will keep on growing in knowledge and understanding. ¹⁰For I want you to understand what really matters, so that you may live pure and blameless lives until the day of Christ's return. ¹¹May you always be filled with the fruit of your salvation—the righteous character produced in your life by Jesus Christ—for this will bring much glory and praise to God.

¹²And I want you to know, my dear brothers and sisters, that everything that has happened to me here has helped to spread the Good News. ¹³For everyone here, including the whole palace guard, knows that I am in chains because of Christ. ¹⁴And because of my imprisonment, most of the believers here have gained confidence and boldly speak God's message without fear.

¹⁵It's true that some are preaching out of jealousy and rivalry. But others preach about Christ with pure motives. ¹⁶They preach because they love me, for they know I have been appointed to defend the Good News. ¹⁷Those others do not have pure motives as they preach about Christ. They preach with selfish ambition, not sincerely, intending

to make my chains more painful to me. [18]But that doesn't matter. Whether their motives are false or genuine, the message about Christ is being preached either way, so I rejoice. And I will continue to rejoice. [19]For I know that as you pray for me and the Spirit of Jesus Christ helps me, this will lead to my deliverance.

[20]For I fully expect and hope that I will never be ashamed, but that I will continue to be bold for Christ, as I have been in the past. And I trust that my life will bring honor to Christ, whether I live or die. [21]For to me, living means living for Christ, and dying is even better. [22]But if I live, I can do more fruitful work for Christ. So I really don't know which is better. [23]I'm torn between two desires: I long to go and be with Christ, which would be far better for me. [24]But for your sakes, it is better that I continue to live.

[25]Knowing this, I am convinced that I will remain alive so I can continue to help all of you grow and experience the joy of your faith. [26]And when I come to you again, you will have even more reason to take pride in Christ Jesus because of what he is doing through me.

[27]Above all, you must live as citizens of heaven, conducting yourselves in a manner worthy of the Good News about Christ. Then, whether I come and see you again or only hear about you, I will know that you are standing together with one spirit and one purpose, fighting together for the faith, which is the Good News. [28]Don't be intimidated in any way by your enemies. This will be a sign to them that they are going to be destroyed, but that you are going to be saved, even by God himself. [29]For you have been given not only the privilege of trusting in Christ but also the privilege of suffering for him. [30]We are in this struggle together. You have seen

my struggle in the past, and you know that I am still in the midst of it.

Chapter 2

Is there any encouragement from belonging to Christ? Any comfort from his love? Any fellowship together in the Spirit? Are your hearts tender and compassionate? [2]Then make me truly happy by agreeing wholeheartedly with each other, loving one another, and working together with one mind and purpose.

[3]Don't be selfish; don't try to impress others. Be humble, thinking of others as better than yourselves. [4]Don't look out only for your own interests, but take an interest in others, too.

[5]You must have the same attitude that Christ Jesus had.

[6]Though he was God,
    he did not think of equality with God
    as something to cling to.
[7]Instead, he gave up his divine privileges;
    he took the humble position of a slave
    and was born as a human being.
When he appeared in human form,
    [8]he humbled himself in obedience to God
    and died a criminal's death on a cross.
[9]Therefore, God elevated him to the place of
      highest honor
    and gave him the name above all other names,
[10]that at the name of Jesus every knee should bow,
    in heaven and on earth and under the earth,
[11]and every tongue declare that Jesus Christ
      is Lord,
    to the glory of God the Father.

[12]Dear friends, you always followed my instructions when I was with you. And now that I am away, it is even more important. Work hard to show the results of your salvation, obeying God with deep reverence and fear. [13]For God is working in you, giving you the desire and the power to do what pleases him.

[14]Do everything without complaining and arguing, [15]so that no one can criticize you. Live clean, innocent lives as children of God, shining like bright lights in a world full of crooked and perverse people. [16]Hold firmly to the word of life; then, on the day of Christ's return, I will be proud that I did not run the race in vain and that my work was not useless. [17]But I will rejoice even if I lose my life, pouring it out like a liquid offering to God, just like your faithful service is an offering to God. And I want all of you to share that joy. [18]Yes, you should rejoice, and I will share your joy.

[19]If the Lord Jesus is willing, I hope to send Timothy to you soon for a visit. Then he can cheer me up by telling me how you are getting along. [20]I have no one else like Timothy, who genuinely cares about your welfare. [21]All the others care only for themselves and not for what matters to Jesus Christ. [22]But you know how Timothy has proved himself. Like a son with his father, he has served with me in preaching the Good News. [23]I hope to send him to you just as soon as I find out what is going to happen to me here. [24]And I have confidence from the Lord that I myself will come to see you soon.

[25]Meanwhile, I thought I should send Epaphroditus back to you. He is a true brother, co-worker, and fellow soldier. And he was your messenger to help me in my need. [26]I am sending him because he has been longing to see you, and he was very distressed that you heard he was ill. [27]And he certainly was ill; in fact, he almost died. But

God had mercy on him—and also on me, so that I would not have one sorrow after another.

²⁸So I am all the more anxious to send him back to you, for I know you will be glad to see him, and then I will not be so worried about you. ²⁹Welcome him in the Lord's love and with great joy, and give him the honor that people like him deserve. ³⁰For he risked his life for the work of Christ, and he was at the point of death while doing for me what you couldn't do from far away.

Chapter 3

Whatever happens, my dear brothers and sisters, rejoice in the Lord. I never get tired of telling you these things, and I do it to safeguard your faith.

²Watch out for those dogs, those people who do evil, those mutilators who say you must be circumcised to be saved. ³For we who worship by the Spirit of God are the ones who are truly circumcised. We rely on what Christ Jesus has done for us. We put no confidence in human effort, ⁴though I could have confidence in my own effort if anyone could. Indeed, if others have reason for confidence in their own efforts, I have even more!

⁵I was circumcised when I was eight days old. I am a pure-blooded citizen of Israel and a member of the tribe of Benjamin—a real Hebrew if there ever was one! I was a member of the Pharisees, who demand the strictest obedience to the Jewish law. ⁶I was so zealous that I harshly persecuted the church. And as for righteousness, I obeyed the law without fault.

⁷I once thought these things were valuable, but now I consider them worthless because of what Christ has done. ⁸Yes, everything else is worthless when compared with the infinite value of knowing Christ Jesus my Lord.

For his sake I have discarded everything else, counting it all as garbage, so that I could gain Christ [9]and become one with him. I no longer count on my own righteousness through obeying the law; rather, I become righteous through faith in Christ. For God's way of making us right with himself depends on faith. [10]I want to know Christ and experience the mighty power that raised him from the dead. I want to suffer with him, sharing in his death, [11]so that one way or another I will experience the resurrection from the dead!

[12]I don't mean to say that I have already achieved these things or that I have already reached perfection. But I press on to possess that perfection for which Christ Jesus first possessed me. [13]No, dear brothers and sisters, I have not achieved it, but I focus on this one thing: Forgetting the past and looking forward to what lies ahead, [14]I press on to reach the end of the race and receive the heavenly prize for which God, through Christ Jesus, is calling us.

[15]Let all who are spiritually mature agree on these things. If you disagree on some point, I believe God will make it plain to you. [16]But we must hold on to the progress we have already made.

[17]Dear brothers and sisters, pattern your lives after mine, and learn from those who follow our example. [18]For I have told you often before, and I say it again with tears in my eyes, that there are many whose conduct shows they are really enemies of the cross of Christ. [19]They are headed for destruction. Their god is their appetite, they brag about shameful things, and they think only about this life here on earth. [20]But we are citizens of heaven, where the Lord Jesus Christ lives. And we are eagerly waiting for him to return as our Savior. [21]He will take our weak mortal bodies and change them into glorious bodies like

his own, using the same power with which he will bring everything under his control.

Chapter 4

Therefore, my dear brothers and sisters, stay true to the Lord. I love you and long to see you, dear friends, for you are my joy and the crown I receive for my work.

²Now I appeal to Euodia and Syntyche. Please, because you belong to the Lord, settle your disagreement. ³And I ask you, my true partner, to help these two women, for they worked hard with me in telling others the Good News. They worked along with Clement and the rest of my co-workers, whose names are written in the Book of Life.

⁴Always be full of joy in the Lord. I say it again—rejoice! ⁵Let everyone see that you are considerate in all you do. Remember, the Lord is coming soon.

⁶Don't worry about anything; instead, pray about everything. Tell God what you need, and thank him for all he has done. ⁷Then you will experience God's peace, which exceeds anything we can understand. His peace will guard your hearts and minds as you live in Christ Jesus.

⁸And now, dear brothers and sisters, one final thing. Fix your thoughts on what is true, and honorable, and right, and pure, and lovely, and admirable. Think about things that are excellent and worthy of praise. ⁹Keep putting into practice all you learned and received from me—everything you heard from me and saw me doing. Then the God of peace will be with you.

¹⁰How I praise the Lord that you are concerned about me again. I know you have always been concerned for me, but you didn't have the chance to help me. ¹¹Not that I was ever in need, for I have learned how to be content with whatever I have. ¹²I know how to live on almost

nothing or with everything. I have learned the secret of living in every situation, whether it is with a full stomach or empty, with plenty or little. [13]For I can do everything through Christ, who gives me strength. [14]Even so, you have done well to share with me in my present difficulty.

[15]As you know, you Philippians were the only ones who gave me financial help when I first brought you the Good News and then traveled on from Macedonia. No other church did this. [16]Even when I was in Thessalonica you sent help more than once. [17]I don't say this because I want a gift from you. Rather, I want you to receive a reward for your kindness.

[18]At the moment I have all I need—and more! I am generously supplied with the gifts you sent me with Epaphroditus. They are a sweet-smelling sacrifice that is acceptable and pleasing to God. [19]And this same God who takes care of me will supply all your needs from his glorious riches, which have been given to us in Christ Jesus.

[20]Now all glory to God our Father forever and ever! Amen.

[21]Give my greetings to each of God's holy people—all who belong to Christ Jesus. The brothers who are with me send you their greetings. [22]And all the rest of God's people send you greetings, too, especially those in Caesar's household.

[23]May the grace of the Lord Jesus Christ be with your spirit.

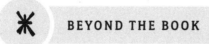

Materialism

Materialism: We are our own individual "gods"; there is no objective god to become, to serve, to submit to, or to dwell with. We simply are.

Authentic materialists trust that the composition of Prime Reality is only that which can be observed and measured materially. No actual spirituality or spiritual realm exists. Humans are beautiful, complex systems of matter and electricity who are subjected to an intricate arrangement of pure cause and effect and are awesomely "aware" of their immediate unfolding presence in time and space. The impression of the ideal is a completely subjective, relative concept. Consistent materialists believe that humans can do and be whatever they prefer, so long as they avoid negative natural consequences while simultaneously and paradoxically acknowledging that this freedom is arbitrary and ultimately a facade; life is actually an unfolding passive adventure of random electric reactionary impulses. Consistent and authentic materialists unabashedly and wholeheartedly embrace that life is ultimately absurd and beautifully or grotesquely ridiculous; therefore, genuine materialists assert that humans can attempt to "create" their own sense of adventure, purpose, and meaning and live out their awareness in the most personally pleasurable ways available while seeking and hoping to achieve positive natural consequences and to avoid negative natural consequences.

Some religions, isms, and ways that construct trust lists from this philosophy:

+ Atheism
+ Humanism
+ Existentialism
+ Phenomenology
+ Nihilism
+ _____
+ _____
+ _____

EXTEND YOUR LEARNING: Find or draw some images to ponder and discuss that relate to this description of materialism.

The Philosophical Trust List of an Authentic Materialist

Fill in the chart with some of the major cultural, religious, social, and personal consequences of adopting the authentic materialist's trust list.

1. What is the Nature of reality? What is really real?	*Only* the material (the natural) is really real; there is no spiritual realm.	
2. Who or what is God?	There is no objective powerful being outside of the material. God is a figment of human creativity and imagination, a creative idea or concept.	

Big Questions of Life	Authentic Materialism	Some Major Cultural, Religious, Social, and Personal Consequences of This Trust List
3. What is a human being? What is humankind? (Who am I? What am I?)	Human beings are fascinating, unique, and highly complex systems of matter and electricity that are beautifully aware of "self" and "others."	
4. What is the basis of and standard for morality? How do I decide between right and wrong, and who or what is the basis for moral authority?	All morality is ultimately subjective and based exclusively or collectively on self, majority, and power.	
5. What happens to humans at death?	Humans cease to be aware of their existence at the point of death.	
6. What is the meaning and purpose of human history? What is the essence of human interaction and relationships?	"History is a linear stream of events linked by cause and effect'"* (such as natural selection). Human inter-action is literally chemistry and pure cause and effect.	
7. Why are we here? Where are we going? What is the purpose of human existence?	Humans get to create their own individual and collective mean-ing for life.	

---

* James Sire, *The Universe Next Door* (Downers Grove, IL: InterVarsity Press, 2009), 80.

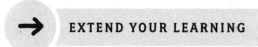

Reality Check for Materialism

Take time to do some (safe) research to see how materialism has influenced the categories below. A good library is best for this, but the Internet, with a good filter, will also be helpful. This critical personal research and discovery will create a firm foundation for discussion when you realize that real people believe these things and live their daily lives based on the answers this philosophy provides. Consider doing a "show and tell" from your research on this worldview.

CULTURAL CONNECTIONS:

_____

_____

_____

_____

_____

_____

_____

POETRY AND BOOKS:

_____

_____

_____

_____

_____

_____

_____

ART/ARTISTS:

_____

_____

_____

_____

_____

_____

_____

FILM:

_____

_____

_____

_____

_____

_____

MUSIC:

_____

_____

_____

_____

_____

_____

_____

RELIGIONS:

_____

_____

_____

_____

_____

_____

_____

SACRED/CORE TEXTS:

_____

_____

_____

_____

_____

_____

_____

HISTORICAL FIGURES:

_____

_____

_____

_____

_____

_____

_____

INFLUENTIAL/FAMOUS PEOPLE:

_____

_____

_____

_____

_____

_____

_____

KEY LANDMARKS/HISTORICAL SIGNIFICANCE:

_____

_____

_____

_____

_____

_____

John Keats and Materialism

"WHEN I HAVE FEARS THAT I MAY CEASE TO BE"

When I have fears that I may cease to be
*   Before my pen has glean'd my teeming brain,*
Before high piled books, in charact'ry.
*   Hold like rich garners the full-ripen'd grain;*
When I behold, upon the night's starr'd face,
*   Huge cloudy symbols of a high romance,*
And think that I may never live to trace
*   Their shadows, with the magic hand of chance;*
And when I feel, fair creature of an hour!
*   That I shall never look upon thee more,*
Never have relish in the faery power
*   Of unreflecting love!—then on the shore*
Of the wide world I stand alone, and think
Till love and fame to nothingness do sink.

1. Take some time and research John Keats, the author of this poem. Born in 1795, Keats was an English Romantic poet and author of many poems, several of which are considered to be among the

finest in the English language. What did you learn about Keats that might inform your reading of this poem?

2. If you were on a walk with Keats or sitting next to him as he was sick, what would you say? Imagine having a conversation with him about this poem and his impending death. What would you ask him about how he came to trust what he trusts about reality? What would you want him to know about your trust list?

EXTEND YOUR LEARNING: Send John Keats a message/ letter as he stands "alone" on the shore of the wide world. If you could send him one letter to read before he dies, what would you want him to know? (Remember our Kingdom community mind-set of love and honor.)

"The Madman" by Friedrich Nietzsche

ANALYZING THE TEXT

German philosopher Friedrich Nietzsche was born in 1844, the son of a pious Lutheran pastor. He wrote several influential works of philosophy, popularizing the idea of the "superman" and the phrase "God is dead" and questioning the influence of religion on modern society.

Read "The Madman" and highlight, annotate, and ponder these famous words. Where do you see connections to the discussions on materialism? The connections you make can be subtle, overt, literary, historical, artistic, personal, biblical, and metaphoric.

Highlight or underline at least three quotes that you find engaging, and be prepared to explain why you picked these quotes.

"THE MADMAN"

The Madman.—Have you ever heard of the madman who on a bright morning lighted a lantern and ran to the market-place calling out unceasingly: "I seek God! I seek God!"—As there were many people standing about who did not believe in God, he caused a great deal of

SPACE TO WRITE OR DOODLE

amusement. Why! is he lost? said one. Has he strayed away like a child? said another. Or does he keep himself hidden? Is he afraid of us? Has he taken a sea-voyage? Has he emigrated?—the people cried out laughingly, all in a hubbub. The insane man jumped into their midst and transfixed them with his glances. "Where is God gone?" he called out. "I mean to tell you! *We have killed him,*—you and I! We are all his murderers! But how have we done it? How were we able to drink up the sea? Who gave us the sponge to wipe away the whole horizon? What did we do when we loosened this earth from its sun? Whither does it now move? Whither do we move? Away from all suns? Do we not dash on unceasingly? Backwards, sideways, forwards, in all directions? Is there still an above and below? Do we not stray, as through infinite nothingness? Does not empty space breathe upon us? Has it not become colder? Does not night come on continually, darker and darker? Shall we not have to light lanterns in the morning? Do we not hear the noise of the grave-diggers who are burying God? Do we not smell the divine putrefaction?—for even Gods putrefy! God is dead! God remains dead! And we have killed him! How shall we console ourselves, the most murderous of all murderers? The holiest and the mightiest that the world has hitherto possessed, has bled to death under our knife,—who will wipe the blood from us? With what water could we cleanse ourselves? What lustrums, what sacred games shall we have to devise? Is not the magnitude of this deed too great for us? Shall we not ourselves have to become Gods, merely to seem worthy of it? There never was a greater event,—and on account of it, all who are born after us belong to a higher history than any history hitherto!"—Here the madman was silent and looked again at his hearers; they also were silent and looked at him in surprise. At last he threw his lantern

on the ground, so that it broke in pieces and was extin-
guished. "I come too early," he then said, "I am not yet at
the right time. This prodigious event is still on its way, and
is travelling,—it has not yet reached men's ears. Lightning
and thunder need time, the light of the stars needs time,
deeds need time, even after they are done, to be seen and
heard. This deed is as yet further from them than the fur-
thest star,—*and yet they have done it!*"—It is further stated
that the madman made his way into different churches on
the same day, and there intoned his *Requiem aeternam deo.*
When led out and called to account, he always gave the
reply: "What are these churches now, if they are not the
tombs and monuments of God?"*

---

* Translated by Thomas Common, from Nietzsche's *The Joyful Wisdom.*

Nietzsche's "Madman" and Me

After reading "The Madman" by Friedrich Nietzsche on pages 163–165 of this guidebook, answer the following questions.

1. What is your personal emotional response to Nietzsche's essay? How do you feel after reading this?

2. Who is the madman in the story? And why is he mad (crazy)? What evidence does Nietzsche provide for the reader to show that he is mad (crazy)?

3. Read 1 Kings 18, the story of Elijah's encounter with the prophets of Baal on Mount Carmel. Now reread the opening paragraph of "The Madman." What connections can you make between the stories? Why do you think Nietzsche is making this connection? What is Nietzsche implying about Christianity in his time? What can our response to Nietzsche's deep call for "fire from heaven" be in our culture?

4. Work in small groups to find three things an authentic materialist could tweet from this essay with the hashtag #madman.

   Tweet #1:

   Tweet #2:

   Tweet #3:

Ecclesiastes and Materialism

ANALYZING THE TEXT

In one sitting, read and annotate these potent words to the citizens of the kingdom of Israel during the reign of King Solomon. Imagine you are a citizen of Solomon's glorious kingdom, where he reigns as an aging king after gaining the reputation as one blessed with divine wisdom from the almighty, true God. Where do you see connections to our discussions on materialism and the religions, ways, and isms that base their trust lists on this philosophical approach to reality? The connections you make can be subtle, overt, literary, historical, artistic, personal, or metaphoric.

Highlight or underline at least three verses that you find engaging, and be prepared to explain why you picked these verses.

SPACE TO
WRITE OR
DOODLE

ECCLESIASTES 1–3 AND 12

Chapter 1

These are the words of the Teacher, King David's son, who ruled in Jerusalem.

²"Everything is meaningless," says the Teacher, "completely meaningless!"

³What do people get for all their hard work under the sun? ⁴Generations come and generations go, but the earth never changes. ⁵The sun rises and the sun sets, then hurries around to rise again. ⁶The wind blows south, and then turns north. Around and around it goes, blowing in circles. ⁷Rivers run into the sea, but the sea is never full. Then the water returns again to the rivers and flows out again to the sea. ⁸Everything is wearisome beyond description. No matter how much we see, we are never satisfied. No matter how much we hear, we are not content.

⁹History merely repeats itself. It has all been done before. Nothing under the sun is truly new. ¹⁰Sometimes people say, "Here is something new!" But actually it is old; nothing is ever truly new. ¹¹We don't remember what happened in the past, and in future generations, no one will remember what we are doing now.

¹²I, the Teacher, was king of Israel, and I lived in Jerusalem. ¹³I devoted myself to search for understanding and to explore by wisdom everything being done under heaven. I soon discovered that God has dealt a tragic existence to the human race. ¹⁴I observed everything going on under the sun, and really, it is all meaningless—like chasing the wind.

¹⁵What is wrong cannot be made right.
   What is missing cannot be recovered.

¹⁶I said to myself, "Look, I am wiser than any of the kings who ruled in Jerusalem before me. I have greater wisdom and knowledge than any of them." ¹⁷So I set out to learn everything from wisdom to madness and folly. But I learned firsthand that pursuing all this is like chasing the wind.

[18]The greater my wisdom, the greater my grief.

To increase knowledge only increases sorrow.

Chapter 2

I said to myself, "Come on, let's try pleasure. Let's look for the 'good things' in life." But I found that this, too, was meaningless. [2]So I said, "Laughter is silly. What good does it do to seek pleasure?" [3]After much thought, I decided to cheer myself with wine. And while still seeking wisdom, I clutched at foolishness. In this way, I tried to experience the only happiness most people find during their brief life in this world.

[4]I also tried to find meaning by building huge homes for myself and by planting beautiful vineyards. [5]I made gardens and parks, filling them with all kinds of fruit trees. [6]I built reservoirs to collect the water to irrigate my many flourishing groves. [7]I bought slaves, both men and women, and others were born into my household. I also owned large herds and flocks, more than any of the kings who had lived in Jerusalem before me. [8]I collected great sums of silver and gold, the treasure of many kings and provinces. I hired wonderful singers, both men and women, and had many beautiful concubines. I had everything a man could desire!

[9]So I became greater than all who had lived in Jerusalem before me, and my wisdom never failed me. [10]Anything I wanted, I would take. I denied myself no pleasure. I even found great pleasure in hard work, a reward for all my labors. [11]But as I looked at everything I had worked so hard to accomplish, it was all so meaningless—like chasing the wind. There was nothing really worthwhile anywhere.

[12]So I decided to compare wisdom with foolishness and madness (for who can do this better than I, the king?).

[13]I thought, "Wisdom is better than foolishness, just as light is better than darkness. [14]For the wise can see where they are going, but fools walk in the dark." Yet I saw that the wise and the foolish share the same fate. [15]Both will die. So I said to myself, "Since I will end up the same as the fool, what's the value of all my wisdom? This is all so meaningless!" [16]For the wise and the foolish both die. The wise will not be remembered any longer than the fool. In the days to come, both will be forgotten.

[17]So I came to hate life because everything done here under the sun is so troubling. Everything is meaningless—like chasing the wind.

[18]I came to hate all my hard work here on earth, for I must leave to others everything I have earned. [19]And who can tell whether my successors will be wise or foolish? Yet they will control everything I have gained by my skill and hard work under the sun. How meaningless! [20]So I gave up in despair, questioning the value of all my hard work in this world.

[21]Some people work wisely with knowledge and skill, then must leave the fruit of their efforts to someone who hasn't worked for it. This, too, is meaningless, a great tragedy. [22]So what do people get in this life for all their hard work and anxiety? [23]Their days of labor are filled with pain and grief; even at night their minds cannot rest. It is all meaningless.

[24]So I decided there is nothing better than to enjoy food and drink and to find satisfaction in work. Then I realized that these pleasures are from the hand of God. [25]For who can eat or enjoy anything apart from him? [26]God gives wisdom, knowledge, and joy to those who please him. But if a sinner becomes wealthy, God takes the wealth away and gives it to those who please him. This, too, is meaningless—like chasing the wind.

Chapter 3

[1]For everything there is a season,
    a time for every activity under heaven.
[2]A time to be born and a time to die.
    A time to plant and a time to harvest.
[3]A time to kill and a time to heal.
    A time to tear down and a time to build up.
[4]A time to cry and a time to laugh.
    A time to grieve and a time to dance.
[5]A time to scatter stones and a time to
        gather stones.
    A time to embrace and a time to turn away.
[6]A time to search and a time to quit searching.
    A time to keep and a time to throw away.
[7]A time to tear and a time to mend.
    A time to be quiet and a time to speak.
[8]A time to love and a time to hate.
    A time for war and a time for peace.

[9]What do people really get for all their hard work? [10]I have seen the burden God has placed on us all. [11]Yet God has made everything beautiful for its own time. He has planted eternity in the human heart, but even so, people cannot see the whole scope of God's work from beginning to end. [12]So I concluded there is nothing better than to be happy and enjoy ourselves as long as we can. [13]And people should eat and drink and enjoy the fruits of their labor, for these are gifts from God.

[14]And I know that whatever God does is final. Nothing can be added to it or taken from it. God's purpose is that people should fear him. [15]What is happening now has happened before, and what will happen in the future has happened before, because God makes the same things happen over and over again.

[16]I also noticed that under the sun there is evil in the courtroom. Yes, even the courts of law are corrupt! [17]I said to myself, "In due season God will judge everyone, both good and bad, for all their deeds."

[18]I also thought about the human condition—how God proves to people that they are like animals. [19]For people and animals share the same fate—both breathe and both must die. So people have no real advantage over the animals. How meaningless! [20]Both go to the same place—they came from dust and they return to dust. [21]For who can prove that the human spirit goes up and the spirit of animals goes down into the earth? [22]So I saw that there is nothing better for people than to be happy in their work. That is our lot in life. And no one can bring us back to see what happens after we die. . . .

Chapter 12

Don't let the excitement of youth cause you to forget your Creator. Honor him in your youth before you grow old and say, "Life is not pleasant anymore." [2]Remember him before the light of the sun, moon, and stars is dim to your old eyes, and rain clouds continually darken your sky. [3]Remember him before your legs—the guards of your house—start to tremble; and before your shoulders—the strong men—stoop. Remember him before your teeth—your few remaining servants—stop grinding; and before your eyes—the women looking through the windows—see dimly.

[4]Remember him before the door to life's opportunities is closed and the sound of work fades. Now you rise at the first chirping of the birds, but then all their sounds will grow faint.

[5]Remember him before you become fearful of falling and worry about danger in the streets; before your hair

turns white like an almond tree in bloom, and you drag along without energy like a dying grasshopper, and the caperberry no longer inspires sexual desire. Remember him before you near the grave, your everlasting home, when the mourners will weep at your funeral.

[6]Yes, remember your Creator now while you are young, before the silver cord of life snaps and the golden bowl is broken. Don't wait until the water jar is smashed at the spring and the pulley is broken at the well. [7]For then the dust will return to the earth, and the spirit will return to God who gave it.

[8]"Everything is meaningless," says the Teacher, "completely meaningless."

[9]Keep this in mind: The Teacher was considered wise, and he taught the people everything he knew. He listened carefully to many proverbs, studying and classifying them. [10]The Teacher sought to find just the right words to express truths clearly.

[11]The words of the wise are like cattle prods—painful but helpful. Their collected sayings are like a nail-studded stick with which a shepherd drives the sheep.

[12]But, my child, let me give you some further advice: Be careful, for writing books is endless, and much study wears you out.

[13]That's the whole story. Here now is my final conclusion: Fear God and obey his commands, for this is everyone's duty. [14]God will judge us for everything we do, including every secret thing, whether good or bad.

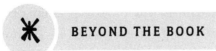

Monism

Monism: We are already part of "god" (the universe); embrace and enjoy this truth and stop striving to become what you already are.

Complete monists trust that both the measurable material and mysterious spiritual realms coexist as one (very large) entity. Monists, often called pantheists, assert that all of reality is one reality presenting itself as "dual" in nature. This duality is represented in unlimited perspectives and polarities as experienced throughout the vast complexity and tensions of life. While humans tend to perceive reality as separated, monists assert that these distinctions are a deception. Due to the perception of separateness, monism is often expressed as or interpreted as "dualism" because the polarities inherent in monism tend to manifest as perceived opposites like good and evil or light and dark. For a complete monist, all of life is connected literally. Humans are part of all existence, and all of that which exists is already the ideal for life and thus is already perfect as various parts of the one entity that monists often refer to as "god." "God" literally is everything, and humans are part of the everything that exists. For all of life, emotions = spirit = god = truth = life = material = perspective. Like a human body, which has many apparent distinctions and parts yet maintains a complex unity and harmony, so is the universal reality and unity of monism. Humans each embody (literally) unique perspectives of god.

Humans have unlimited potential and power as god or as a connected part of god. Humans can embrace their unique preferences and seek a balance of all perspectives and polarities so as to wake up, realize, and utilize their true identity and literal unity. Humans (along with all creatures and all parts of reality) can grow in awareness of all perspectives as they embody the simplicity and complexity of life as part of the one self. Humans can learn how to see all of life and all of life's tensions and polarities—the dualities of life—as a valid and valuable part of humanity's oneness, collective unity, and coexistence with all that exists.

Some religions, isms, and ways that construct trust lists from this philosophy:

+ Pantheism
+ "New Age"
+ Much of Hinduism
+ Tribal religions that worship nature
+ Theosophy
+ "Dualism"
+ _____
+ _____
+ _____

EXTEND YOUR LEARNING: Find or draw some images to ponder and discuss that relate to this description of monism.

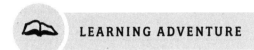
The Philosophical Trust List of a Complete Monist

Fill in the chart with some of the major cultural, religious, social, and personal consequences of adopting the complete monist's trust list.

Big Questions of Life	Complete Monism	Some Major Cultural, Religious, Social, and Personal Consequences of This Trust List
1. What is the nature of reality? What is really real?	The spiritual and the material are *both* really real, existing as one entity. Reality presents itself as dual in nature, yet all of existence is ultimately one interconnected unity.	
2. Who or what is God?	Everything is "god." Everything and everybody in the universe is an integral, interconnected part of the unity of life called "god."	

Big Questions of Life	Complete Monism	Some Major Cultural, Religious, Social, and Personal Consequences of This Trust List
3. What is a human being? What is humankind? (Who am I? What am I?)	Humans are unique, unrepeatable parts of "god"; we are part of the one body of the universe and the entirety of reality referred to as "god."	
4. What is the basis of and standard for morality? How do I decide between right and wrong, and who or what is the basis for moral authority?	Morality is completely subjective based on one's individual preference as a part of the interconnected universal reality called "god," and thus morality is relative.	
5. What happens to humans at death?	When we die, we "morph" into another part of exis- tence and another com- ponent of the universal reality, which is "god."	
6. What is the meaning and purpose of human history? What is the essence of human interaction and relationships?	History and human memory consist of the repository of collective memories of our collective coexistence as "god."	
7. Why are we here? Where are we going? What is the purpose of human existence?	Every human has the exciting opportunity to continue experiencing being various components of universal reality—of "god"—forever.	

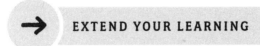

Reality Check for Monism

Take time to do some (safe) research to see how monism has influenced the categories below. A good library is best for this, but the Internet, with a good filter, will also be helpful. This critical personal research and discovery will create a firm foundation for discussion when you realize that real people believe these things and live their daily lives based on the answers this philosophy provides. Consider doing a "show and tell" from your research on this worldview.

CULTURAL CONNECTIONS:

_____

_____

_____

_____

_____

_____

_____

POETRY AND BOOKS:

_____

_____

_____

_____

_____

_____

_____

ART/ARTISTS:

_____

_____

_____

_____

_____

_____

_____

FILM:

_____

_____

_____

_____

_____

_____

MUSIC:

_____

_____

_____

_____

_____

_____

_____

RELIGIONS:

_____

_____

_____

_____

_____

_____

SACRED/CORE TEXTS:

_____

_____

_____

_____

_____

_____

HISTORICAL FIGURES:

_____

_____

_____

_____

_____

_____

_____

INFLUENTIAL/FAMOUS PEOPLE:

_____

_____

_____

_____

_____

_____

KEY LANDMARKS/HISTORICAL SIGNIFICANCE:

_____

_____

_____

_____

_____

_____

Monism and "The Egg"

Read the short story "The Egg" by Andy Weir.* Write a personal reader response to this unique story. A traditional reader response comes in two parts. First, give your immediate response to what you read. Second, give an analytical response to why you think you responded the way you initially did. One of the keys to this story is that there is only one being with two voices. It looks like a dialogue, but it is a monologue. One way to wrap your brain around this is to imagine that you can have a conversation with yourself when you were five and ten years old. There is only one "you," but each day there is a different version of you. Welcome to monism, if this concept is taken to a global scale.

EXTEND YOUR LEARNING: Research what motivated Andy Weir to write this story. Find and share other stories or poems that reflect on monism.

---

* At the time of this writing, this is available online at the author's website: http://www.galactanet.com/oneoff/theegg
_mod.html.

PART 1: YOUR IMMEDIATE RESPONSE TO READING THIS STORY.

PART 2: YOUR THOUGHTFUL, REFLECTIVE, AND ANALYTICAL RESPONSE TO THIS STORY AND MONISM.

1 John and Monism

ANALYZING THE TEXT

Read and annotate 1 John, written by the apostle John, as an essay in one sitting. Pretend you are hearing it for the first time just years after Jesus has come back from the dead. Where do you see connections to our discussion on monism and the religions, ways, and isms that base their trust lists on this philosophical approach to reality? The connections you make can be subtle, overt, literary, historical, artistic, personal, or metaphoric.

Highlight or underline at least three verses that you find engaging, and be prepared to explain why you picked these verses.

1 JOHN

Chapter 1

We proclaim to you the one who existed from the beginning, whom we have heard and seen. We saw him with our own eyes and touched him with our own hands. He is the Word of life. ²This one who is life itself was revealed to us, and we have seen him. And now we testify and proclaim

SPACE TO
WRITE OR
DOODLE

185

to you that he is the one who is eternal life. He was with the Father, and then he was revealed to us. [3]We proclaim to you what we ourselves have actually seen and heard so that you may have fellowship with us. And our fellowship is with the Father and with his Son, Jesus Christ. [4]We are writing these things so that you may fully share our joy.

[5]This is the message we heard from Jesus and now declare to you: God is light, and there is no darkness in him at all. [6]So we are lying if we say we have fellowship with God but go on living in spiritual darkness; we are not practicing the truth. [7]But if we are living in the light, as God is in the light, then we have fellowship with each other, and the blood of Jesus, his Son, cleanses us from all sin.

[8]If we claim we have no sin, we are only fooling ourselves and not living in the truth. [9]But if we confess our sins to him, he is faithful and just to forgive us our sins and to cleanse us from all wickedness. [10]If we claim we have not sinned, we are calling God a liar and showing that his word has no place in our hearts.

Chapter 2

My dear children, I am writing this to you so that you will not sin. But if anyone does sin, we have an advocate who pleads our case before the Father. He is Jesus Christ, the one who is truly righteous. [2]He himself is the sacrifice that atones for our sins—and not only our sins but the sins of all the world.

[3]And we can be sure that we know him if we obey his commandments. [4]If someone claims, "I know God," but doesn't obey God's commandments, that person is a liar and is not living in the truth. [5]But those who obey God's word truly show how completely they love him. That is how we know we are living in him. [6]Those who say they live in God should live their lives as Jesus did.

[7]Dear friends, I am not writing a new commandment for you; rather it is an old one you have had from the very beginning. This old commandment—to love one another—is the same message you heard before. [8]Yet it is also new. Jesus lived the truth of this commandment, and you also are living it. For the darkness is disappearing, and the true light is already shining.

[9]If anyone claims, "I am living in the light," but hates a fellow believer, that person is still living in darkness. [10]Anyone who loves a fellow believer is living in the light and does not cause others to stumble. [11]But anyone who hates a fellow believer is still living and walking in darkness. Such a person does not know the way to go, having been blinded by the darkness.

[12]I am writing to you who are God's children
   because your sins have been forgiven through
   Jesus.
[13]I am writing to you who are mature in the faith
   because you know Christ, who existed from the
   beginning.
I am writing to you who are young in the faith
   because you have won your battle with the
   evil one.
[14]I have written to you who are God's children
   because you know the Father.
I have written to you who are mature in the faith
   because you know Christ, who existed from the
   beginning.
I have written to you who are young in the faith
   because you are strong.
God's word lives in your hearts,
   and you have won your battle with the evil one.

[15]Do not love this world nor the things it offers you, for when you love the world, you do not have the love of the Father in you. [16]For the world offers only a craving for physical pleasure, a craving for everything we see, and pride in our achievements and possessions. These are not from the Father, but are from this world. [17]And this world is fading away, along with everything that people crave. But anyone who does what pleases God will live forever.

[18]Dear children, the last hour is here. You have heard that the Antichrist is coming, and already many such antichrists have appeared. From this we know that the last hour has come. [19]These people left our churches, but they never really belonged with us; otherwise they would have stayed with us. When they left, it proved that they did not belong with us.

[20]But you are not like that, for the Holy One has given you his Spirit, and all of you know the truth. [21]So I am writing to you not because you don't know the truth but because you know the difference between truth and lies. [22]And who is a liar? Anyone who says that Jesus is not the Christ. Anyone who denies the Father and the Son is an antichrist. [23]Anyone who denies the Son doesn't have the Father, either. But anyone who acknowledges the Son has the Father also.

[24]So you must remain faithful to what you have been taught from the beginning. If you do, you will remain in fellowship with the Son and with the Father. [25]And in this fellowship we enjoy the eternal life he promised us.

[26]I am writing these things to warn you about those who want to lead you astray. [27]But you have received the Holy Spirit, and he lives within you, so you don't need anyone to teach you what is true. For the Spirit teaches you everything you need to know, and what he teaches is

true—it is not a lie. So just as he has taught you, remain in fellowship with Christ.

[28]And now, dear children, remain in fellowship with Christ so that when he returns, you will be full of courage and not shrink back from him in shame.

[29]Since we know that Christ is righteous, we also know that all who do what is right are God's children.

Chapter 3

See how very much our Father loves us, for he calls us his children, and that is what we are! But the people who belong to this world don't recognize that we are God's children because they don't know him. [2]Dear friends, we are already God's children, but he has not yet shown us what we will be like when Christ appears. But we do know that we will be like him, for we will see him as he really is. [3]And all who have this eager expectation will keep themselves pure, just as he is pure.

[4]Everyone who sins is breaking God's law, for all sin is contrary to the law of God. [5]And you know that Jesus came to take away our sins, and there is no sin in him. [6]Anyone who continues to live in him will not sin. But anyone who keeps on sinning does not know him or understand who he is.

[7]Dear children, don't let anyone deceive you about this: When people do what is right, it shows that they are righteous, even as Christ is righteous. [8]But when people keep on sinning, it shows that they belong to the devil, who has been sinning since the beginning. But the Son of God came to destroy the works of the devil. [9]Those who have been born into God's family do not make a practice of sinning, because God's life is in them. So they can't keep on sinning, because they are children of God. [10]So now we can tell who are children of God and who are children of

the devil. Anyone who does not live righteously and does not love other believers does not belong to God.

[11]This is the message you have heard from the beginning: We should love one another. [12]We must not be like Cain, who belonged to the evil one and killed his brother. And why did he kill him? Because Cain had been doing what was evil, and his brother had been doing what was righteous. [13]So don't be surprised, dear brothers and sisters, if the world hates you.

[14]If we love our brothers and sisters who are believers, it proves that we have passed from death to life. But a person who has no love is still dead. [15]Anyone who hates another brother or sister is really a murderer at heart. And you know that murderers don't have eternal life within them.

[16]We know what real love is because Jesus gave up his life for us. So we also ought to give up our lives for our brothers and sisters. [17]If someone has enough money to live well and sees a brother or sister in need but shows no compassion—how can God's love be in that person?

[18]Dear children, let's not merely say that we love each other; let us show the truth by our actions. [19]Our actions will show that we belong to the truth, so we will be confident when we stand before God. [20]Even if we feel guilty, God is greater than our feelings, and he knows everything.

[21]Dear friends, if we don't feel guilty, we can come to God with bold confidence. [22]And we will receive from him whatever we ask because we obey him and do the things that please him.

[23]And this is his commandment: We must believe in the name of his Son, Jesus Christ, and love one another, just as he commanded us. [24]Those who obey God's commandments remain in fellowship with him, and he with them. And we know he lives in us because the Spirit he gave us lives in us.

Chapter 4

Dear friends, do not believe everyone who claims to speak by the Spirit. You must test them to see if the spirit they have comes from God. For there are many false prophets in the world. [2]This is how we know if they have the Spirit of God: If a person claiming to be a prophet acknowledges that Jesus Christ came in a real body, that person has the Spirit of God. [3]But if someone claims to be a prophet and does not acknowledge the truth about Jesus, that person is not from God. Such a person has the spirit of the Antichrist, which you heard is coming into the world and indeed is already here.

[4]But you belong to God, my dear children. You have already won a victory over those people, because the Spirit who lives in you is greater than the spirit who lives in the world. [5]Those people belong to this world, so they speak from the world's viewpoint, and the world listens to them. [6]But we belong to God, and those who know God listen to us. If they do not belong to God, they do not listen to us. That is how we know if someone has the Spirit of truth or the spirit of deception.

[7]Dear friends, let us continue to love one another, for love comes from God. Anyone who loves is a child of God and knows God. [8]But anyone who does not love does not know God, for God is love.

[9]God showed how much he loved us by sending his one and only Son into the world so that we might have eternal life through him. [10]This is real love—not that we loved God, but that he loved us and sent his Son as a sacrifice to take away our sins.

[11]Dear friends, since God loved us that much, we surely ought to love each other. [12]No one has ever seen God. But if we love each other, God lives in us, and his love is brought to full expression in us.

[13]And God has given us his Spirit as proof that we live in him and he in us. [14]Furthermore, we have seen with our own eyes and now testify that the Father sent his Son to be the Savior of the world. [15]All who declare that Jesus is the Son of God have God living in them, and they live in God. [16]We know how much God loves us, and we have put our trust in his love.

God is love, and all who live in love live in God, and God lives in them. [17]And as we live in God, our love grows more perfect. So we will not be afraid on the day of judgment, but we can face him with confidence because we live like Jesus here in this world.

[18]Such love has no fear, because perfect love expels all fear. If we are afraid, it is for fear of punishment, and this shows that we have not fully experienced his perfect love. [19]We love each other because he loved us first.

[20]If someone says, "I love God," but hates a fellow believer, that person is a liar; for if we don't love people we can see, how can we love God, whom we cannot see? [21]And he has given us this command: Those who love God must also love their fellow believers.

Chapter 5

Everyone who believes that Jesus is the Christ has become a child of God. And everyone who loves the Father loves his children, too. [2]We know we love God's children if we love God and obey his commandments. [3]Loving God means keeping his commandments, and his commandments are not burdensome. [4]For every child of God defeats this evil world, and we achieve this victory through our faith. [5]And who can win this battle against the world? Only those who believe that Jesus is the Son of God.

[6]And Jesus Christ was revealed as God's Son by his baptism in water and by shedding his blood on the

cross—not by water only, but by water and blood. And the Spirit, who is truth, confirms it with his testimony. [7]So we have these three witnesses—[8]the Spirit, the water, and the blood—and all three agree. [9]Since we believe human testimony, surely we can believe the greater testimony that comes from God. And God has testified about his Son. [10]All who believe in the Son of God know in their hearts that this testimony is true. Those who don't believe this are actually calling God a liar because they don't believe what God has testified about his Son.

[11]And this is what God has testified: He has given us eternal life, and this life is in his Son. [12]Whoever has the Son has life; whoever does not have God's Son does not have life.

[13]I have written this to you who believe in the name of the Son of God, so that you may know you have eternal life. [14]And we are confident that he hears us whenever we ask for anything that pleases him. [15]And since we know he hears us when we make our requests, we also know that he will give us what we ask for.

[16]If you see a fellow believer sinning in a way that does not lead to death, you should pray, and God will give that person life. But there is a sin that leads to death, and I am not saying you should pray for those who commit it. [17]All wicked actions are sin, but not every sin leads to death.

[18]We know that God's children do not make a practice of sinning, for God's Son holds them securely, and the evil one cannot touch them. [19]We know that we are children of God and that the world around us is under the control of the evil one.

[20]And we know that the Son of God has come, and he has given us understanding so that we can know the true

God. And now we live in fellowship with the true God because we live in fellowship with his Son, Jesus Christ. He is the only true God, and he is eternal life.

[21]Dear children, keep away from anything that might take God's place in your hearts.

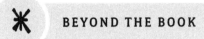

BEYOND THE BOOK

Theism

Religious theism: We are unique individual creations hoping to become perfect (or complete) so as to dwell with God, our perfect Creator.

Religious theists trust that both the spiritual and the material are components of Prime Reality, and while these components are interdependent and independent with one another, they are also mysteriously intradependent, dependent with each other. Humans are unique individual creations in the image of a free, independent, personal, and all-powerful Creator, often referred to as God. Although humans are created in the image of the one perfect God as distinct individual creations of God, humans are actually independent beings from God and do not possess the exact nature of God. Humans are created to dwell freely with God and enjoy a relationship with God and God's creation. On earth, humans exist as imperfect (incomplete) beings, essentially separated from God's perfect identity and standards. Therefore, in order for humans to escape eternal separation from their perfect Creator and to dwell perpetually with their perfect Creator, individual perfection (fullness) must be achieved and sustained.

Some religions, isms, and ways that construct trust lists from this philosophy:

+ Judaism
+ Islam
+ Christianity
+ Tribal religions that worship a Creator
+ _____
+ _____
+ _____

EXTEND YOUR LEARNING: Find or draw some images to ponder and discuss that relate to this description of religious theism.

The Philosophical Trust List of a Religious Theist

Fill in the chart with some of the major cultural, religious, social, and personal consequences of adopting the religious theist's trust list.

Big Questions of Life	Religious Theism	Some Major Cultural, Religious, Social, and Personal Consequences of This Trust List
1. What is the nature of reality? What is really real?	The spiritual and the material are *both* real yet independent, interdependent, and intradependent with each other.	• Indebent ⊙WN realm disting • Intrdependen connected • Intrgdlpnil redlu
2. Who or what is God?	There is a distinct God that is the all-powerful Creator, sustainer, and giver of all of life. God is personal and has personality.	

Big Questions of Life	Religious Theism	Some Major Cultural, Religious, Social, and Personal Consequences of This Trust List
3. What is a human being? What is humankind? (Who am I? What am I?)	Humans are a distinct, wonderful creation made in the image of God but not possessing the exact nature of God or existing as an extension or part of God.	
4. What is the basis of and standard for morality? How do I decide between right and wrong, and who or what is the basis for moral authority?	All ethical morality is objective based on the personal, all-powerful nature of God, who is perfect and good. God (and God's word and nature) is the standard for and author of morality.	
5. What happens to humans at death?	When we die, we obtain individual perfection and exist eternally in continual relationship with the perfect personal God, or we remain in an imperfect, incomplete state and necessarily exist separated from God.	
6. What is the meaning and purpose of human history? What is the essence of human interaction and relationships?	History is a "linear, meaningful sequence of events leading to the fulfillment of God's purposes for humanity" in an open system.* History is the true, epic adventure story of God's interaction with humankind.	
7. Why are we here? Where are we going? What is the purpose of human existence?	At least one reason that humans exist is to enjoy and experience a meaningful relationship with the Creator and Sustainer of life.	

---

* James Sire, *The Universe Next Door* (Downers Grove, IL: InterVarsity Press, 2009), 22–23.

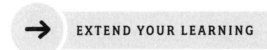

Reality Check
for Religious Theism

Take time to do some (safe) research to see how religious theism has influenced the categories below. A good library is best for this, but the Internet, with a good filter, will also be helpful. This critical personal research and discovery will create a firm foundation for discussion when you realize that real people believe these things and live their daily lives based on the answers this philosophy provides. Consider doing a "show and tell" from your research on this worldview.

CULTURAL CONNECTIONS:

_____

_____

_____

_____

_____

_____

_____

POETRY AND BOOKS:

_____

_____

_____

_____

_____

_____

_____

ART/ARTISTS:

_____

_____

_____

_____

_____

_____

FILM:

_____

_____

_____

_____

_____

_____

MUSIC:

_____

_____

_____

_____

_____

_____

_____

RELIGIONS:

_____

_____

_____

_____

_____

_____

SACRED/CORE TEXTS:

_____

_____

_____

_____

_____

_____

_____

HISTORICAL FIGURES:

_____

_____

_____

_____

_____

_____

_____

INFLUENTIAL/FAMOUS PEOPLE:

_____

_____

_____

_____

_____

_____

_____

KEY LANDMARKS/HISTORICAL SIGNIFICANCE:

_____

_____

_____

_____

_____

_____

_____

A Discussion of "I Love You and Buddha Too"

Listen to or watch the Mason Jennings song "I Love You and Buddha Too."

1. There is a lot of love mentioned in the song. What do you believe is the chief goal or purpose of this declaration and all the various kinds of love mentioned in this song? Write down some of the catchy lines in the song.

2. The main question in this song is: "Why do some people say there is just one way?"

   + What are various potential answers to this bold question?

+ What is your personal answer to this question?

+ Who are the "some people" the narrator is referring to?

+ What are some of the answers that "some people" are known to give?

3. In his Gospel, the apostle John quotes Jesus saying, "I am the way, the truth, and the life. No one can come to the Father except through me" (John 14:6). Why is this considered a controversial and exclusive claim?

+ What new philosophical insights are gained or lost by interpreting the words "the Father" to mean "perfection"?

+ Why *philosophically* and *theologically* is Jesus' statement not rude or exclusive?

+ What are the implications if Jesus had said instead, "I am a way, but there are other valid ways. I am a truth among many truths. I am a form of life. Anyone can get to the Father or achieve perfection however they so choose, but I am a pretty good option"?

"The Inch"

From the book (page 102):

To highlight this freedom and relationship and to illustrate
how humans are unique creations of a God with being
and personality (not just consciousness or a state of being),
I consider the painting of the *Creation of Adam* from the
ceiling of the Sistine Chapel. I know that this is distinctly
Christian, but the metaphor would work for anyone who has
a theistic worldview. In the painting there is a very muscular,
bearded God hovering in a red backdrop and surrounded by
chubby cherubs, extending his arm out and down to an equally
muscular Adam who is reposed on something like a rock.
The most essential piece of the painting for our purposes here
is the inch of separation and distinction. These two beings
are almost touching but not quite. There is relationship in
their eyes, facial expression, reach, and movement. There are
obvious distinctions such as beard and garment. But what
are most powerful to me are the similarities. I can't tell who

has the bigger biceps or quads; they both have eyes, ears, and mouths. They look like they could wrestle, converse, go for a walk, and share a tasty beverage or scrumptious meal together. They look like they could be best friends and talk until the sun comes up or maybe not talk at all. Adam and God could hug if they wanted to. A Buddhist cannot hug nirvana, and a Hindu cannot have a conversation and a meal with Brahma. I am not saying that in theism God will necessarily hug you, share a conversation with you, or enjoy a meal with you. Nevertheless, in theism God is a relational being, and in order for God to have relationship, there must be something to have a relationship with.

Find a picture of *Creation of Adam* from the ceiling of the Sistine Chapel. Draw or paste representations for the hands and fingers below to represent each worldview. What happens to the "inch" if the hands were to represent the four different worldviews?

IDEALISM

A shadow fouching a shadow

MATERIALISM

You touching your morality

MONISM

God touching God

THEISM

God touching You

The Gospel of John and Theism

ANALYZING THE TEXT

Find a Bible and read the Gospel of John as a long essay in one sitting. (If possible, find a translation different from the one you usually read. Even better, find one without chapter and verse numbers.) Pretend you are hearing this for the first time as a true story about the man Jesus. Where do you see connections to our discussion on theism, especially the religions, ways, and isms that base their trust lists on this philosophical approach to reality? The connections you make can be subtle, overt, literary, historical, artistic, personal, or metaphoric. Record these connections on the next page, and be prepared to share them.

Also on the next page, write down at least three verses that you find engaging, and briefly explain why you picked these verses. Cut and paste or write out the entire verse—do not simply put the reference. Do not summarize the verses as a response.

THE GOSPEL OF JOHN NOTES

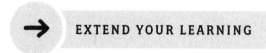
The Big Questions: An Interview

Interview a friend or neighbor. As you do so, remember these core values: Ask. Listen. Honor. Connect. Learn. Love.

THE PHILOSOPHICAL TRUST LIST OF _____

1. What is the nature of reality? What is really real?

2. Who or what is God?

3. What is a human being? What is humankind? (Who am I? What am I?)

4. What is the basis of and standard for morality? How do I decide between right and wrong, and who or what is the basis of moral authority?

5. What happens to humans at death?

6. What is the meaning and purpose of human history? What is the essence of human interaction and relationships?

7. Why are we here? Where are we going? What is the purpose of human existence?

The Big Questions: Another Interview

Interview another friend or neighbor.

THE PHILOSOPHICAL TRUST LIST OF _____

1. What is the nature of reality? What is really real?

2. Who or what is God?

3. What is a human being? What is humankind? (Who am I? What am I?)

4. What is the basis of and standard for morality? How do I decide between right and wrong, and who or what is the basis of moral authority?

5. What happens to humans at death?

6. What is the meaning and purpose of human history? What is the essence of human interaction and relationships?

7. Why are we here? Where are we going? What is the purpose of human existence?

Part Two Projects

Consider doing one of the following projects to extend your learning of part 2 concepts.

ACADEMIC LETTER

Write a letter to G. K. Chesterton or C. S. Lewis that incorporates a description of key portions of your spiritual journey synthesized with how it has changed or been enlightened or enhanced due your interaction with part 1 and part 2 of the *Inklings on Philosophy and Worldview* book and your philosophical studies of the nature of reality, Chesterton's *Orthodoxy*, and Lewis's *Mere Christianity*. The language you choose for the letter should be respectful and academic. You are to pretend that Lewis and Chesterton are alive and well. The genres you may choose from include a very personal letter or a formal letter to a professional writer.

DIALOGUE

Create a dialogue. Clearly explain the overarching context of the conversation, the underlying worldviews and personalities of the characters, and the immediate characteristics of the setting and issue(s) being discussed. The dialogue should be between at least three characters representing three philosophies, with one character who represents the Christian theistic philosophy. Remember, in the book we have explored the power of language and the potential of conversation. Work hard to make the discussion meaningful, and be sure to have a beginning, middle, and conclusion. It will help to pick an issue or two to discuss in the assignment or to address a few of the philosophy questions from your notes. Be sure to include an explanatory introduction and cite your quotes on a works cited page. Optional extension: turn this dialogue into a formal debate on this topic.

COLLAGE/SCRAPBOOK

Create a quotations and images collage or scrapbook for philosophy, *Orthodoxy*, and *Mere Christianity*. The goal of this assignment is to creatively incorporate images, photographs, and artwork that represent selected quotes and passages to express a theme or interconnected themes from what we have been studying. Use at least ten quotes from *Mere Christianity* or *Orthodoxy* specifically synthesized with ten quotes on philosophy and the nature of reality from other sources and at least seven images. Be sure to include a two-to-three-paragraph explanatory introduction and cite your quotes on a works cited page.

CREATIVE THEATRICAL/VIDEO PROJECT

Write a scenario or scene that can be acted out live or turned into a video that unpacks one or several aspects of the big questions of philosophy and how the four worldviews answer these questions. Consider setting this scenario in a relevant situation that involves your community. You could also create four "commercials" that try to convert people to each worldview. Be sure to create these scenes and "commercials" with the utmost dignity, integrity, love, and honor. This is a great chance to flesh out the Kingdom community values. These could also be presented as dramatic readings. Optional extension: find various movie clips or theatrical presentations that display the four different worldviews.

Christ: The Fullness of Reality

Christ is the visible image of the invisible God.
    He existed before anything was created and
        is supreme over all creation,
for through him God created everything. . . .
    Everything was created through him
        and for him.
He existed before anything else,
    and he holds all creation together.

COLOSSIANS 1:15-17

Outline

These questions are essential to our learning and growth for this course of study. They are the focus of part 3 of the *Inklings on Philosophy and Worldview* book and the driving force behind this guidebook. The book, your instruction, the supplemental podcasts (available at IntheTrueMyth.org), and the assignments in this guidebook are all developed to help you answer these questions:

1. How is Christ the fullness of reality?
2. Why is Jesus essential to an authentic trinitarian worldview?
3. Why is grace essential to Jesus and a Christ-centered biblical worldview?
4. What are key consequences of trusting varying answers to the seven core questions of philosophy?
5. What is authentic biblical grace and salvation through grace, and what makes grace so unique in the context of the fractured version of the four worldviews?
6. Why is paradox essential for a Christ-centered biblical worldview?
7. How can I use Lewis's moral argument in book 1 of *Mere Christianity* to come to a trustworthy God-centered worldview?

8. How can I use Lewis's book 2 of *Mere Christianity* to come to a trustworthy Christ-centered worldview?

9. Why is Jesus' way the best way to live?

10. Where do we see truth revealed, and how can we connect truth in the four dominant worldviews and their trust lists?

11. How is Christ at the center of philosophy and worldview studies?

12. What is an incarnational worldview?

13. Why is Jesus essential to an authentic incarnational worldview?

14. What is perichoresis as a worldview?

15. What does it mean to have an "encounter with the living God"?

16. What does it mean to get beyond philosophy, religion, and stories into an authentic, loving relationship with Christ?

PART THREE SUGGESTED READINGS

○ All of part 3 from the *Inklings on Philosophy and Worldview* book (pages 113–195)

○ G. K. Chesterton: "The Paradoxes of Christianity" (pages 257–282)

○ C. S. Lewis: *Mere Christianity* books 1 and 2 (supplemental)

○ Romans 1–8 (pages 288–306)

○ C. S. Lewis: The Chronicles of Narnia (supplemental)

PART THREE LEARNING OPPORTUNITIES

Learning Adventures

○ A Christ-Centered Incarnational Worldview (pages 225–226)

○ Silly Strips and Fractured Truth (pages 227–228)

○ The Trinity, the Chandelier, and Chesterton's "Silly Strips" (pages 234–236)

○ The Power of Paradox (pages 283–284)

○ The Parable of Grace: Reflection and Discussion (pages 316–317)

○ "This Is Not a Pipe": Reflection and Discussion (pages 322–323)

○ The Encounter (pages 324–327)

O The Invitation to Love (pages 331–332)
O The Power of Love (pages 333–336)

Extend Your Learning

O The Last Supper (pages 229–230)
O Your Philosophical House (page 256)
O *Mere Christianity* and Evidence for God (pages 285–287)
O *The Case for Christ* Movie and Story (pages 307–310)
O *The Truman Show* and You (pages 318–319)
O The Aslan Moment (pages 328–330)

Exploring Ideas

O "The Paradoxes of Christianity" from G. K. Chesterton's *Orthodoxy* (pages 257–282)
O Romans 1–8 and *Mere Christianity* (pages 288–306)

Beyond the Book

O The Chandelier (pages 231–234)
O Lights On and Off: Pure Idealism (pages 237–240)
O Lights On and Off: Authentic Materialism (pages 241–245)
O Lights On and Off: Complete Monism (pages 246–250)
O Lights On and Off: Religious Theism (pages 251–255)
O A Potential Trust List for a Christ-Centered Theist (pages 311–312)
O The Parable of Grace (pages 313–315)
O "This Is Not a Pipe" (pages 320–321)

Coordinates and Bearings for Learning Adventures: Part Three

Part 3 is meant to guide you to the destination of clearly seeing that Christ is the fullness of reality and consequently how to have a Christ-centered, biblical worldview. This is to be accomplished through understanding that all the truths in other worldviews point us to the truth of Christ, thus allowing each of us to honor and lovingly engage other worldviews with grace and truth. Grace and truth are the operative means for communication and interaction with all people and all worldviews.

This section of the guidebook is also meant to guide you beyond (but not disregarding) religion, philosophy, theology, and worldview into an *authentic, intimate, loving relationship with the living, triune God.* On this part of the journey, it is essential that we learn that Truth is a person, a living being—the living being of Jesus Christ—and not just a concept. This section will also guide you to move from the shadows of belief into a solid identity and understanding of our invitation into the Kingdom of God here and now, as beloved sons and daughters of the true King!

This section of your learning journey will focus on and invite you into . . .

+ Seeing some of the profound consequences for dividing
  Prime Reality.
+ Knowing that the power of paradox is essential for comprehending
  Christ as the fullness of reality.
+ Understanding that C. S. Lewis's moral argument for the existence
  of God is accomplished without using Scripture.
+ Comprehending C. S. Lewis's perspective on why trust in *Jesus* is
  essential as opposed to simply believing in a theistic "God."
+ Grasping the nature and essence of free will and several
  compelling reasons why God created free will.
+ Articulating biblical grace and why Jesus saves humans by grace.
+ Understanding how biblical grace makes a Christ-centered
  biblical worldview unique among all of the worldviews,
  religions, and isms.
+ Experiencing truth as a person, not just a concept.
+ Heeding John's call to lovingly "test the spirits" in order to
  maintain awareness of the Holy Spirit's movements and to
  maintain a sustainable, authentic, loving relationship with
  the real Christ.
+ Recognizing and responding to the innate desire to be authentically
  loved by God and to the call to truly love God and others as the
  ultimate motivator and goal for us on our worldview quest.

PART 3 SUMMARY

Part 3 puts the worldview "strips" back together and examines Christ
as the fullness of reality. The truth from each of the four worldviews
is put together, seamlessly, in him. We humans work so hard to make
our one piece or strip of Prime Reality into the entirety. We stretch it
to try to make it fit every question or issue or reality we encounter, but
only in Christ do we find both complete truth and complete grace.
And only in the power of paradox do we find the freedom and integrity
to live in harmony with the life-giving tensions implicit within Prime
Reality.

This section examines embracing the tensions of the paradoxes of Christ, for paradox is the only way to make sense of what we encounter in the world. Belief in Christ as the real truth requires an acceptance of mystery and wonder. Trusting in not only a Christ-centered biblical worldview but trusting in the person of Christ requires embracing paradox. It also requires embracing the Truth as a living, loving, relational being rather than as a philosophical construct or a religious system.

A Christ-Centered Incarnational Worldview

There is a huge and heroic sanity of which moderns can only collect the fragments. There is a giant of whom we see only the lopped arms and legs walking about. They have torn the soul of Christ into silly strips, labelled egoism and altruism, and they are equally puzzled by his insane magnificence and his insane meekness. They have parted his garments among them, and for his vesture they have cast lots; though the coat was without seam woven from the top throughout.

G. K. CHESTERTON, *ORTHODOXY*

1. What are the "silly strips" Chesterton refers to?

2. What "silly strips" are you holding on to? What will it take to see the whole instead of just your strip?

3. Can you think of someone who is clinging to a single strip, thinking it's the whole picture? What strip is it, and why do they view it that way?

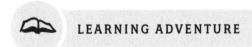

Silly Strips and Fractured Truth

In Tolkien's epic Lord of the Rings series, Aragorn inherits a powerful sword ("Narsil") that was used to fight the enemy Sauron. While this sword was used once upon a time to defeat Sauron, the battle fractured it into several shards. It's easy to see that this is a complete sword, just broken into pieces. Each piece on its own isn't completely trustworthy, or particularly useful, but it is an authentic part of the whole, original "Narsil." In The Lord of the Rings, the sword is reforged and accompanies Aragorn on his new quest to defeat Sauron.

This can be a potent visual representation of a fractured worldview. The "silly strips" that Chesterton refers to are Christ. I think it is valuable and convicting to apply this metaphor to God's Word, and swords are a great image for this. After all, the apostle Paul clearly says that "the sword of the Spirit" is the "word of God" (Ephesians 6:17), and the author of Hebrews calls Scripture "sharper than the sharpest two-edged sword" (Hebrews 4:12). The metaphor of a shattered sword can represent any time we use Scripture and prophecy (God's word to us through the Holy Spirit) out of context and fracture the truth they contain.

1. Draw a representation of the shards of Narsil as a potent reminder of fractured truth.

2. On your own and in small groups, list at least three ways over the past two thousand years that people have fractured the Word of God. What consequences have resulted from splintering not just Christ but also his words?

3. After you have recognized a fracturing of God's Word, what can you do to piece the Word of God back together?

The Last Supper

Find and print two copies of Leonardo da Vinci's *The Last Supper* painting online. Cut one copy into four sections and paste them on the next page, where indicated. Label each section with one of the four worldviews: idealism, materialism, monism, and theism. Then paste your copy of the full painting where indicated. Read and discuss chapter 14 of the *Inklings on Philosophy and Worldview* book (pages 121–124).

1. What truth have you cut out of your "picture" of Prime Reality? How might this distort your perception of the fullness of Christ?

2. Make a list of the truths from each worldview under each section of the painting. Consider how these truths can work together to form the truth and fullness of reality as found in Christ.

WE HAVE CHOPPED UP THE MASTERPIECE . . .

[Glue your chopped-up painting here]

. . . BUT EACH STRIP IS STILL A PIECE OF THE ORIGINAL.

[Glue a copy of the original here.]

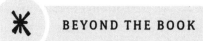

The Chandelier

The chandelier is a visual representation of how all four worldviews inter-mingle and, through paradox, create the area for truth to exist. There are apparent opposites on each side that create space in which each concept operates. For example, notice "objectivity" and its opposite "relativity": the two must balance each other for truth to be expressed. Think of basic morality. There are so many things that easily fall into the camp of moral relativity and are often considered cultural, such as what we set as speed limits, styles of clothing, and the food we eat or do not eat. Rape, murder, stealing, and child abuse can easily be seen to be ethically, objectively evil. The truth is found in having hardline objective morality balanced with culturally relative standards. The truth of reality is lost when we turn off one idea or the other. We would not want it that way, we would find it ridiculous, and we would lose an obvious truth if we tried to say that all of our moral decisions were objective truths. The same is true if we were to say that all of morality is cultural and relative.

The same truth is evident for "unity" and "distinction." If we have no distinctions from each other and God, then we lose not only the concept of "self"; we actually lose ourselves. If we are completely independent and distinct from one another and God, then we lose our sense of unity and community, and we also lose our obvious reliance upon our Creator and our need for God. How can we even pretend to exist on our own for more than eighty to one hundred years without sustaining eternal life provided by the giver and sustainer of life? How easily we forget that as a human family, we are all connected by the material fabric of our world and the unifying Spirit of Christ, who is immanent and omnipresent. It is a well-established scientific fact that we are more similar than we are different.

The diagram on the next page shows all four circles intermingling and balancing one another—this is the expression of a complete, balanced truth. In a paradox, there will be tension between the seeming opposites. However, when we try to resolve that tension (and thus resolve the paradox), we will lose the truth found in the balance between the truths.

As you turn the individual lights of the chandelier on and off, different perspectives or worldviews are revealed. In the next several readings and assignments, let's take a look at how that works. Remember that one of the keys to the truth embedded within this metaphor is that the sum of the whole is greater than the parts combined.

The main goal of this section of the workbook is to create a repository of information to start or continue conversations on the real and often potent consequences of the various trust lists.

What follows is an organic, but not exhaustive, list of the complexities of the costs and the benefits of trusting various answers to the seven big questions used in this book. It is meant to be thought-provoking and conversation worthy. Feel free to disagree, debate, dialogue, discuss, and differentiate. This type of information is helpful when you are trying to figure out what you believe or to start the journey of understanding why others might have a different answer on their trust list than the one on yours. Everybody trusts something. Of course, there is a cost to that choice, but there are benefits as well—otherwise, no human would trust it. In our conversation with people of different worldviews, many people see only the negatives of the other side. It can be invaluable to look for the benefits in other options and trust lists as you assess your own.

In addition to the "lights on and off," for each of the ways the four worldviews answer the seven big questions, I've included a third example of how the view of truth that each worldview claims is taken up into "Christ, the fullness of reality." Remember, these examples are simply meant to get you started. Use these first steps to go deeper into your understanding. There is an invitation at the end of Part 3 to take these concepts further and find more places where the fullness of Christ is revealed in the four worldviews.

All of life is a journey, and we are all at different places on our journey. Much of the adventure is filled with perpetually learning how to renew our minds and learning how to think differently. It all starts with learning how to trust something and even Someone new, not just with our heads but also with our hearts and, ultimately, with our whole beings. This takes time, dialogue, thoughtful contemplation, surrender, outside help, and the vital process of being on the journey of a lifetime.

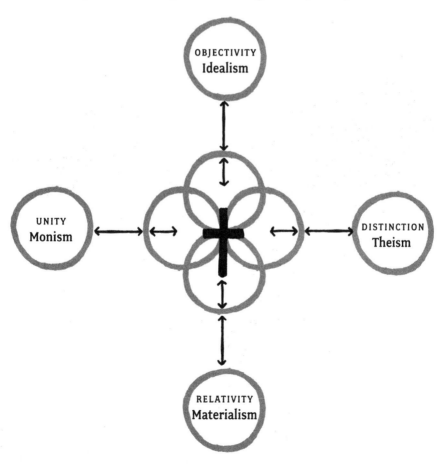

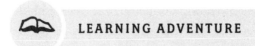
The Trinity, the Chandelier, and Chesterton's "Silly Strips": Reflection and Discussion

This learning adventure explores and builds upon the concepts found specifically on pages 180–185 of the *Inklings* book. The culmination of the chandelier metaphor is to help us see Christ as the fullness of reality as seen in the powerful paradox of the Triune God, three in one: Father, Son, and Holy Spirit. To see this more fully, it can be helpful to ground the concept in specific truths that point us to this big view of our big God. One helpful way to begin this specific journey is to find various aspects of the Trinity in the isolated worldviews. This learning adventure and journey of discovery starts at the quote found on page 180 of the book: "But when our view of Christ encompasses and honors both spiritual and material reality, the truths from the four worldviews are found in one complete whole: Christ! In him all four 'strips' of the painting are joined together: idealism's truth of the spiritual world and the perfect, objective ideal; materialism's truth of the physical world and the individualism and relativity of humans; monism's truth of the unity and connectedness of all things; and theism's truth of the relational distinction between God and humanity. All these truths are 'held' in Christ. In him, all the lights of the chandelier are on."

A reflective reading of the Nicene Creed is a great way to get this adventure started. You may also want to use the chapters in part 3 of the *Inklings on Philosophy and Worldview* book, the chandelier images, and pages 237–255 in this guidebook to answer and discuss the following topics.

1. Where can we see attributes of God the Father in the "isolated light" and "silly strip" of the eternal spiritual reality and perfected objectivity of idealism?

2. Where can we see attributes of God the Son in the "isolated light" and "silly strip" of the reality of the physical world, the individual, and the general relativity of materialism?

3. Where can we see attributes of God the Holy Spirit in the "isolated light" and "silly strip" of the unity and connectedness of monism?

4. Where can we see attributes of the image of God (*imago dei) in* the "isolated light" and "silly strip" of the relational distinction of religious theism?

5. Where is there truth revealed about various aspects of the Trinity in each of the four worldviews? Where is there "light" in all of the worldviews? (The activity with *The Last Supper* painting [pages 229–230] should help with this activity and learning adventure.)

6. In this context, what might it mean that Jesus says, "I am the light of the world" (John 8:12)?

Lights On and Off: Pure Idealism

Consider the lights on (benefits) and lights off (consequences) of idealism's answers to the seven big worldview questions. Consider also how the truth of idealism is caught up in "Christ, the fullness of reality."

1. WHAT IS THE NATURE OF REALITY? WHAT IS REALLY REAL?

A pure idealist trusts that only the spiritual is really real and reality is a state of eternal, spiritual perfection. The material realm is an imperfect, incomplete, shadowy replica of the ideal.

+ OFF: Individual humans do not currently exist physically. Any existence we might posit is in the form of potential or striving to become one with the ideal.
+ ON: The pain, suffering, and chaos of this world make sense in light of a perfect world that exists independent of this broken one.
+ CHRIST: "Against its will, all creation was subjected to God's curse. But with eager hope, the creation looks forward to the day when it will join God's children in glorious freedom from death and decay" (Romans 8:20-21).

2. WHO OR WHAT IS GOD?

A pure idealist trusts that the impersonal, eternal, perfect, one ideal is what people call "god." It is absolute and complete truth, beauty, and goodness. God is a state of mind and a state of existence. God is the ideal one who is perfect, absolutely and forever. God is the ideal state of being that is the pursuit of humanity.

+ OFF: God is not a being with whom a person can have a relationship. The perfect cannot be truly understood by humans in our current imperfect state.
+ ON: The brokenness, chaos, suffering, and pain of the world make sense in light of our search for the ideal that has yet to be understood by us in our current material state.
+ CHRIST: Jesus Christ, Immanuel ("God with us"), "full of grace and truth" (John 1:14, NIV), has shown us what God is like and has revealed God to us.

3. WHAT IS A HUMAN BEING? WHAT IS HUMANKIND? (WHO AM I? WHAT AM I?)

A pure idealist trusts that humans are not perfect; they are one of the infinite, incomplete shadows of the real state of spiritual perfection. Humans exist simply as potential to become one with the ideal and to finally exist as the perfected ideal in a state of eternal, spiritual perfection and completeness.

+ OFF: You are simply one of the infinite, imperfect, broken images of the perfect existence.
+ ON: Our imperfection explains our brokenness and pain and the tensions of this chaotic world.
+ CHRIST: "Everyone has sinned; we all fall short of God's glorious standard" (Romans 3:23).

4. WHAT IS THE BASIS OF AND STANDARD FOR MORALITY? HOW DO I DECIDE BETWEEN RIGHT AND WRONG, AND WHO OR WHAT IS THE BASIS FOR MORAL AUTHORITY?

A pure idealist trusts that all morality is objective, based on the nature of the impersonal, perfect spiritual ideal, which is absolute truth, perfect beauty, and complete goodness. All thought and behavior is aimed at achieving and sustaining this state of existence.

+ OFF: You do not get to decide what is right and wrong based on your personal preference.
+ ON: Right and wrong behavior is definable based on the objective nature of the perfect, good, and true standard.
+ CHRIST: God, as Creator, sets the rules according to his perfect nature. "Now you must be holy in everything you do, just as God who chose you is holy" (1 Peter 1:15).

5. WHAT HAPPENS TO HUMANS AT DEATH?

A pure idealist trusts that when humans die, perfection is attained and unity with the ideal is achieved. Humans realize their potential, let go of the imperfect representation of self, and become one with the state of spiritual perfection. They cease to exist as imperfect selves and shadowy, broken representations of perfection. They cease to exist materially on earth. Individually, humans cease to exist at all. In essence, real life/true existence begins at death.

+ OFF: You either cease to exist because you become god, or you cease to exist because you are not perfect.
+ ON: You cease to exist as imperfect. Because you relinquished your prior identity and you have achieved perfection and unity with the perfect one, you literally become one with god.
+ CHRIST: "We know that when this earthly tent we live in is taken down (that is, when we die and leave this earthly body), we will have a house in heaven, an eternal body made for us by God himself and not by human hands. . . . Yes, we are fully confident, and we would rather be away from these earthly bodies, for then we will be at home with the Lord" (2 Corinthians 5:1, 8).

6. WHAT IS THE MEANING AND PURPOSE OF HUMAN HISTORY? WHAT IS THE ESSENCE OF HUMAN INTERACTION AND RELATIONSHIPS?

A pure idealist trusts that history and memory are a record of humans striving to escape nonexistence and attain an ideal state of spiritual perfection. Human interaction is summed up and actualized in striving to escape nonexistence, either alone or together.

+ OFF: History is full of shadows, suffering, and striving to become real.

+ ON: You can learn what not to do and try to imitate those who have made it.

+ CHRIST: "Therefore, since we are surrounded by such a huge crowd of witnesses to the life of faith, let us strip off every weight that slows us down, especially the sin that so easily trips us up. And let us run with endurance the race God has set before us" (Hebrews 12:1).

7. WHY ARE WE HERE? WHERE ARE WE GOING? WHAT IS THE PURPOSE OF HUMAN EXISTENCE?

A pure idealist trusts that humans exist only to achieve and sustain an ideal state of spiritual perfection, to escape painful nonexistence, and to exist eternally through becoming absorbed into/unified with the spiritual ideal, which is absolutely and perfectly good, beautiful, and true.

+ OFF: Life is continual striving and suffering in painful awareness of nonexistence, ending in nothingness. You are going nowhere.

+ ON: You can achieve perfection and escape suffering and can eventually exist eternally as perfection.

+ CHRIST: "Our present troubles are small and won't last very long. Yet they produce for us a glory that vastly outweighs them and will last forever!" (2 Corinthians 4:17).

Lights On and Off: Authentic Materialism

Consider the lights on (benefits) and lights off (consequences) of materialism's answers to the seven big worldview questions. Consider also how the truth of materialism is caught up in "Christ, the fullness of reality."

1. WHAT IS THE NATURE OF REALITY? WHAT IS REALLY REAL?

An authentic materialist trusts that only the material (the natural) is really real; there is no spiritual realm. Matter and electricity have existed eternally in various forms and states without beginning or end. What is observable and measurable is really real.

+ OFF: Only what is physically measurable is real.
+ ON: We can attempt to measure, define, and predict reality.
+ CHRIST: "The heavens proclaim the glory of God. The skies display his craftsmanship" (Psalm 19:1).

2. WHO OR WHAT IS GOD?

An authentic materialist trusts that there is no objective, powerful being outside of the material. God is a lovely or ugly lie, a figment of human creativity and imagination, or a generative reactive idea or concept.

+ OFF: There is no all-powerful, perfect, objective being who bestows morality, eternal identity, and objective meaning on our existence. Undeniable, unexplainable, and unpredictable supernatural phenomena cause tension.

+ ON: You are already god and you make up your own concept of perfect. There is no objective, all-powerful, spiritual authority to hold you ultimately accountable for your actions or thoughts. There is no hell and no punishment by god now or after death.

+ CHRIST: God has granted humans autonomy, and while God has set standards for human living, we are free and creative beings, made in the image of our Creator. And thus, God told humanity to "fill the earth and govern it. Reign over the fish in the sea, the birds in the sky, and all the animals that scurry along the ground" (Genesis 1:28).

3. WHAT IS A HUMAN BEING? WHAT IS HUMANKIND? (WHO AM I? WHAT AM I?)

An authentic materialist trusts that a human being is a fascinating, unique, and highly complex system of matter and electricity that is uniquely aware of self and others. Humankind is currently the pinnacle of existence in an infinitely intricate system of cause and effect. Humankind is the amazing realization of the ongoing potential of matter and electricity.

+ OFF: You exist as long as your body lasts and as long as you are aware of your existence. You are simply a complex chemical reaction responding to your environment and various stimuli. Just as a computer has no free will or ability to make independent choices, you are not free either. Your life is cause and effect.

+ ON: Life is relatively predictable and measurable, and pain and suffering are explainable in scientific and medical terms.

+ CHRIST: God's standards are not a moving target, nor does the material world act according to whim. Scripture continually reminds us that we will "reap what we sow" (see, for example,

Galatians 6:7, NIV). Proverbs describes God "set[ting] the limits of the seas" and "mark[ing] off the earth's foundations" (8:29). Humans are the pinnacle of his creation (see Genesis 1:26-31; 2:7; Psalm 8).

4. WHAT IS THE BASIS OF AND STANDARD FOR MORALITY? HOW DO I DECIDE BETWEEN RIGHT AND WRONG, AND WHO OR WHAT IS THE BASIS FOR MORAL AUTHORITY?

An authentic materialist trusts that all morality is ultimately subjective and based on self, majority, and/or power. Morality is essentially absurd at the core. There is no truly objective standard for good and evil for humans, nor could there ever be.

+ OFF: Objective, ultimate morality is absurd. Good and evil, right and wrong behavior are subject to personal preference, power, or majority. Morality is reduced to cause and effect in a closed system.

+ ON: If you can make the electrical, material system of existence work for your personal benefit, you can do anything you like, guilt-free. There are no personal, postmortem consequences for any of your actions or thoughts.

+ CHRIST: Humans are free to make their own decisions as autonomous creatures (see John 8:36). However, the Bible teaches that "each of us will give a personal account to God" (Romans 14:12; see also Ecclesiastes 12:14).

5. WHAT HAPPENS TO HUMANS AT DEATH?

An authentic materialist trusts that humans cease to be aware of their existence at the point of death. There is no eternal existence of a person's "soul" beyond the grave because there is no eternal soul dwelling in the human body. Real life ends at death.

+ OFF: If your existence is pleasurable, it is over when you die. You cease to exist and your awareness stops. There is no eternal awareness or existence as god or with a personal god.

244 ❖ INKLINGS ON PHILOSOPHY AND WORLDVIEW GUIDEBOOK

+ ON: If your existence is miserable, it is over when you die.
  You cease to exist and your awareness stops. There is no eternal
  awareness or existence of separation from a loving and personal
  god. There are no negative eternal consequences for not being
  perfect.

+ CHRIST: Our bodies are valuable to God, such that the future
  hope of Christianity is resurrection: "Our dying bodies must be
  transformed into bodies that will never die" (1 Corinthians 15:53).

6. WHAT IS THE MEANING AND PURPOSE OF HUMAN HISTORY? WHAT IS THE ESSENCE OF HUMAN INTERACTION AND RELATIONSHIPS?

An authentic materialist trusts that humans, individually or collectively, create their own meaning for existence. History and memory are ultimately absurd with no objective, overarching meaning or purpose.

+ OFF: There is no meaning to anything. Events happen and unfold
  in a closed system and history is absurd. Tensions arise from the
  inexplicable or the absurdity of chance defining our lives.

+ ON: Actions have predictable consequences. You can learn from
  cause and effect.

+ CHRIST: The actions you take have an effect beyond your own
  life. God tells Moses, for example, that when one person sins,
  "the entire family is affected—even children in the third and
  fourth generations" (Exodus 34:7).

7. WHY ARE WE HERE? WHERE ARE WE GOING? WHAT IS THE PURPOSE OF HUMAN EXISTENCE? WHAT IS THE PURPOSE OF LIVING FOR TOMORROW?

An authentic materialist trusts that humans create their own meaning for life. At the core, life is essentially, objectively absurd because no objective meaning or purpose does or can exist.

+ OFF: Life is completely absurd and void of any objective
  meaning. Everyone else can also do whatever they desire even if
  it negatively affects you.

+ ON: Life is completely absurd and void of any objective meaning. Have a blast and do whatever you like. Avoid negative personal consequences, live guilt-free, and create your own meaning.

+ CHRIST: God desires our good (see Romans 8:28), and the purpose of life—to be with God—is a joyful state (see Psalm 84). "That's the whole story. Here now is my final conclusion: Fear God and obey his commands, for this is everyone's duty" (Ecclesiastes 12:13).

Lights On and Off:
Complete Monism

Consider the lights on (benefits) and lights off (consequences) of monism's answers to the seven big worldview questions. Consider also how the truth of monism is caught up in "Christ, the fullness of reality."

1. WHAT IS THE NATURE OF REALITY? WHAT IS REALLY REAL?

A complete monist trusts that the spiritual and the material are both real, existing as one entity. The spiritual realm and material realm both exist, but they are one and the same. What we call distinctions and separation are illusory; there is no actual separation or distinction.

+ OFF: You are not an independent human being; there is no real concept of self. All awareness of self is as a piece of god.
+ ON: You are and have always been eternal and you are connected to everything called god. You have unlimited potential as god.
+ CHRIST: "I can do everything through Christ, who gives me strength" (Philippians 4:13). "Christ is the visible image of the invisible God. . . . Everything was created through him and for him. He existed before anything else, *and he holds all creation together*" (Colossians 1:15-17, emphasis added).

2. WHO OR WHAT IS GOD?

A complete monist trusts that everything is god. Everything and everybody in the universe is an integral, interconnected part of the unity of life called god. Existence and reality are what people often call god. God has a dual nature in essence and in being.

+ OFF: There is no all-powerful, perfect, objective being who bestows morality, eternal identity, and objective meaning onto our existence.
+ ON: You are already perfect; you are already god. As god, you have unlimited potential, and nothing is impossible.
+ CHRIST: God is separate from us, but God has made human beings in his image, and Jesus "became human and made his home among us" (John 1:14). God is immanent, as David notes: "I can never escape from your Spirit! I can never get away from your presence!" (Psalm 139:7).

3. WHAT IS A HUMAN BEING? WHAT IS HUMANKIND? (WHO AM I? WHAT AM I?)

A complete monist trusts that humans are unique, unrepeatable parts of god. Humanity is part of the body of the universe and the entirety of reality appropriately referred to as god. The spiritual component to reality resides within, flows through, and permeates every human. Humans are not truly distinct and separate from god, but humans exist as part of the material and spiritual reality of the cosmos, which, in essence, is part of the entire being of god.

+ OFF: You are not an independent human being. There is no real concept of self; all awareness of self is as a piece of god.
+ ON: You are and have always been eternal, and you are connected to everything called god. You have unlimited potential as god, and you are a unique, unrepeatable part of god.
+ CHRIST: Paul writes to believers, "Your body is the temple of the Holy Spirit, who lives in you and was given to you by God"

(1 Corinthians 6:19). Paul also directly invites us into unity and harmony in the Holy Spirit in 1 Corinthians 12. Here is one of many verses: "All of you together are Christ's body, and each of you is a part of it" (verse 27).

4. WHAT IS THE BASIS OF AND STANDARD FOR MORALITY? HOW DO I DECIDE BETWEEN RIGHT AND WRONG, AND WHO OR WHAT IS THE BASIS FOR MORAL AUTHORITY?

A complete monist trusts that morality is completely subjective, based solely on one's individual preference as a part of the interconnected, universal reality called god. Like god (as god is manifested in the universe), morality is dual in nature.

+ OFF *AND* ON: Objective, ultimate morality is absurd. Good and evil do not exist except as descriptive words. Right and wrong behavior is open to personal preference because everyone is part of god. Morality is a description of whatever happens as part of the infinite impulses and expressions of the existence of god. Evil does not exist because all behavior is a part of god.
+ CHRIST: "Work hard to show the results of your salvation, obeying God with deep reverence and fear. For God is working in you, giving you the desire and the power to do what pleases him" (Philippians 2:12-13).

5. WHAT HAPPENS TO HUMANS AT DEATH?

A complete monist trusts that when a human dies, that person morphs into another part of existence and another component of reality, which is god. The shared, united soul shifts into another part of the cosmos with another unique perspective on living as god.

+ OFF: If your existence is pleasurable, it is over when you die. You cease to exist as your current part of god. There is no eternal life as yourself with an objective, loving, relational god.
+ ON: Death does not exist. Death is simply a transformation into another opportunity to exist as another part of god perpetually.

+ CHRIST: There is life after physical death—the unrighteous "will go away to eternal punishment, but the righteous will go into eternal life" (Matthew 25:46).

6. WHAT IS THE MEANING AND PURPOSE OF HUMAN HISTORY? WHAT IS THE ESSENCE OF HUMAN INTERACTION AND RELATIONSHIPS?

A complete monist trusts that history and memory consist of the repository of the memories of our collective coexistence as god. Humans are connected to history as part of the eternally unfolding story of the cosmos (which is god).

+ OFF *AND* ON: You are literally a part of all history and can connect with your own past.
+ CHRIST: You are "part of the eternally unfolding story of the cosmos," but it is God's story, and he invites you to be part of it (see Hebrews 11–12).

7. WHY ARE WE HERE? WHERE ARE WE GOING? WHAT IS THE PURPOSE OF HUMAN EXISTENCE? WHAT IS THE PURPOSE OF LIVING FOR TOMORROW?

A complete monist trusts that every human has the exciting opportunity to continually experience being various components of universal reality—of god—forever. Each human is here to wake up to who he or she is as a unique part of god and reach full potential as a distinct part of the divine existence and unity of god.

+ OFF: Life is completely absurd and void of any objective meaning. Everyone else can also do whatever they desire as god, and they can use the state of being god as the reason for their behavior. Pain, suffering, and trauma are part of god and thus not bad or evil; they just are. There is no good and evil or right and wrong.
+ ON: Life is completely hopeful and yet void of any objective meaning. Have a blast and do whatever you like. Embrace your current status and all experiences in life as god. Live guilt-free

and create your own meaning. Life is never over. You can do whatever you want because everything is personal preference.

+ CHRIST: "We boast in the hope of the glory of God. Not only so, but we also glory in our sufferings, because we know that suffering produces perseverance; perseverance, character; and character, hope. And hope does not put us to shame, because God's love has been poured out into our hearts through the Holy Spirit, who has been given to us" (Romans 5:2-5, NIV).

Lights On and Off: Religious Theism

Consider the lights on (benefits) and lights off (consequences) of theism's answers to the seven big worldview questions. Consider also how the truth of theism is caught up in "Christ, the fullness of reality."

1. WHAT IS THE NATURE OF REALITY? WHAT IS REALLY REAL?

A sincere theist trusts that the spiritual and the material are both real, yet they are independent of and interdependent on each other. The spiritual realm and material realm are both independently real, yet they coexist and interact independently of, interdependently on, and intradependently within each other in various forms and degrees and in diverse ways.

- + OFF: You are not a part of God; rather, you are a limited creation of God.
- + ON: You have an eternal, independent existence as a self. The joy and beauty of this world make sense in light of a perfect world that also exists alongside this one.
- + CHRIST: "We are citizens of heaven, where the Lord Jesus Christ lives. And we are eagerly waiting for him to return as

our Savior. He will take our weak mortal bodies and change them into glorious bodies like his own, using the same power with which he will bring everything under his control" (Philippians 3:20-21).

2. WHO OR WHAT IS GOD?

A religious theist trusts that there is a God who is the all-powerful Creator, the sustainer, and the giver of all life. God is perfect and essentially good in nature and being. God is personal and has a personality. God has full authority. God is the standard for and author of morality.

+ OFF: You are not God, nor will you ever be God. You are currently an imperfect version of yourself. By necessity, you are unable to be in the presence of the perfect God, who—by implication of having a perfect nature—has perfect standards for relationships.

+ ON: There is an all-powerful, perfect, objective being who bestows morality, eternal identity, and objective meaning onto our existence. Undeniable, unexplainable, and unpredictable supernatural phenomena do not cause negative tension. God is personal and loving and desires to dwell with the perfect version of you now and forever.

+ CHRIST: "Christ is the visible image of the invisible God. He existed before anything was created and is supreme over all creation, for through him God created everything in the heavenly realms and on earth. . . . For God in all his fullness was pleased to live in Christ" (Colossians 1:15-16, 19).

3. WHAT IS A HUMAN BEING? WHAT IS HUMANKIND? (WHO AM I? WHAT AM I?)

A religious theist trusts that humans are distinct yet dependent, wonderful creations made in the image of God, or at least capable of some type of meaningful relationship with God; however, humans do not possess the exact nature of God, nor do they exist as only an extension or merely a part of God.

+ OFF: You are not a part of God. You are a limited creation of God. You are currently an imperfect, broken, free being who has fallen from perfection and exists separated from God.

+ ON: You have an eternal, independent existence as a self. The pain and chaos and joy and beauty of this world make sense in light of God's perfect standards. You are an imperfect, broken, yet free being who has fallen from perfection, who can choose to attain perfection or acquire perfection from God.

+ CHRIST: "When I look at the night sky and see the work of your fingers—the moon and the stars you set in place—what are mere mortals that you should think about them, human beings that you should care for them? Yet you made them only a little lower than God and crowned them with glory and honor" (Psalm 8:3-5).

4. WHAT IS THE BASIS OF AND STANDARD FOR MORALITY? HOW DO I DECIDE BETWEEN RIGHT AND WRONG, AND WHO OR WHAT IS THE BASIS FOR MORAL AUTHORITY?

A religious theist trusts that all ethical morality is objective, based on the personal, all-powerful nature of God, who is perfect and good. God is the standard for and author of morality, as are God's Word and God's nature. Though this does not necessarily have to, this may include ritual traditions or cultural norms—what many would call "ritual morality," which is uniquely distinct from ethical morality.

+ OFF: You do not get to decide what is right and wrong based on your personal preference.

+ ON: Good and evil in this world make sense because they are based on the objective nature of the perfect, good, true, loving, and personal God. Right and wrong behavior is definable and comprehensible.

+ CHRIST: "The LORD has told you what is good, and this is what he requires of you: to do what is right, to love mercy, and to walk humbly with your God" (Micah 6:8).

5. WHAT HAPPENS TO HUMANS AT DEATH?

A religious theist trusts that when a human dies, one of two things will occur based on God's and the human's choices in this life. Either the person will obtain or will have received individual perfection and exist eternally in continual relationship with the perfect, personal God, or this person will remain in an imperfect, incomplete state and necessarily exist separated from God.

+ OFF: There is the possibility of an eternal separation from the loving and perfect God.
+ ON: You get to dwell with the perfect, loving, and good God as your actualized, perfect version of yourself.
+ CHRIST: "I heard a loud shout from the throne, saying, 'Look, God's home is now among his people! He will live with them, and they will be his people. God himself will be with them. He will wipe every tear from their eyes, and there will be no more death or sorrow or crying or pain. All these things are gone forever'" (Revelation 21:3-4).

6. WHAT IS THE MEANING AND PURPOSE OF HUMAN HISTORY? WHAT IS THE ESSENCE OF HUMAN INTERACTION AND RELATIONSHIPS?

A religious theist trusts that history is the true, epic adventure story of God's interaction with humankind. It is the real story humans are in right now. Humans are independent and dependent, possessing will and identity as self in communion with others.

+ OFF: You and I are not in control of interpreting the past for our own personal agendas.
+ ON: God is the author and focus of history, and it is a story God is writing and has already written.
+ CHRIST: The Bible is the story of God's relationship with humanity, and through Jesus and participation in his church, we are still in the story of God's work in the world. This is why Jesus instructs us to pray, "May your Kingdom come soon. May your will be done on earth, as it is in heaven" (Matthew 6:10).

7. WHY ARE WE HERE? WHERE ARE WE GOING? WHAT IS THE PURPOSE OF HUMAN EXISTENCE? WHAT IS THE PURPOSE OF LIVING FOR TOMORROW?

A religious theist trusts that at least one primary reason humans exist is to enjoy and experience some form of a meaningful relationship with the Creator and sustainer of life. For Christian theists, humans exist in order to expand, enjoy, and protect God's Kingdom. They exist to bring joy and honor to God and self through genuine worship of God; through loving, healthy relationships with God and others; and through the authentic serving of God and others.

+ OFF: You do not get to create your own meaning. If a person chooses not to be in a personal relationship with God, or if a person chooses not to submit to God as the ultimate authority on morality, there are severe, negative consequences.

+ ON: You exist to do what you were created to do: love God and love others. If you choose to submit to God's authority and plan for your existence, you can receive personal self-actualization, joy, and existence in a meaningful, personal relationship with your Creator. You have eternal purpose and meaning given to you by a loving, all-powerful, personal, perfect, objective God.

+ CHRIST: "God saved you by his grace when you believed. And you can't take credit for this; it is a gift from God. Salvation is not a reward for the good things we have done, so none of us can boast about it. For we are God's masterpiece. He has created us anew in Christ Jesus, so we can do the good things he planned for us long ago" (Ephesians 2:8-10).

Your Philosophical House

Imagine yourself as a living house. God comes in to rebuild that house. At first, perhaps, you can understand what He is doing. He is getting the drains right and stopping the leaks in the roof and so on; you knew that those jobs needed doing and so you are not surprised. But presently He starts knocking the house about in a way that hurts abominably and does not seem to make any sense. What on earth is He up to? The explanation is that He is building quite a different house from the one you thought of—throwing out a new wing here, putting on an extra floor there, running up towers, making courtyards. You thought you were going to be made into a decent little cottage: but He is building a palace. He intends to come and live in it Himself.

C. S. LEWIS, *MERE CHRISTIANITY*

Using this C. S. Lewis quote, consider what your own philosophical house might look like. Use craft supplies, clay, a drawing app, Lego blocks, a 3D printer, or whatever materials you prefer to create some sort of philosophical worldview dwelling place. Label the foundation, the walls, the floors, the windows, and so on using the various tools and terms you have been learning about in the guidebook.

"The Paradoxes of Christianity" from G. K. Chesterton's *Orthodoxy*

ANALYZING THE TEXT

In this chapter, G. K. Chesterton explores the explanatory powers of the Christian view by examining the concept of a paradox. Be sure to annotate this passage as you read it: mark interesting passages, highlight questions that you have, and mark points of particular agreement or disagreement. Find the "gold."

"THE PARADOXES OF CHRISTIANITY"

The real trouble with this world of ours is not that it is an unreasonable world, nor even that it is a reasonable one. The commonest kind of trouble is that it is nearly reasonable, but not quite. Life is not an illogicality; yet it is a trap for logicians. It looks just a little more mathematical and regular than it is; its exactitude is obvious, but its inexactitude is hidden; its wildness lies in wait. I give one coarse instance of what I mean. Suppose some mathematical creature from the moon were to reckon up the human body; he would at once see that the essential thing about

SPACE TO
WRITE OR
DOODLE

it was that it was duplicate. A man is two men, he on the right exactly resembling him on the left. Having noted that there was an arm on the right and one on the left, a leg on the right and one on the left, he might go further and still find on each side the same number of fingers, the same number of toes, twin eyes, twin ears, twin nostrils, and even twin lobes of the brain. At last he would take it as a law; and then, where he found a heart on one side, would deduce that there was another heart on the other. And just then, where he most felt he was right, he would be wrong.

It is this silent swerving from accuracy by an inch that is the uncanny element in everything. It seems a sort of secret treason in the universe. An apple or an orange is round enough to get itself called round, and yet is not round after all. The earth itself is shaped like an orange in order to lure some simple astronomer into calling it a globe. A blade of grass is called after the blade of a sword, because it comes to a point; but it doesn't. Everywhere in things there is this element of the quiet and incalculable. It escapes the rationalists, but it never escapes till the last moment. From the grand curve of our earth it could easily be inferred that every inch of it was thus curved. It would seem rational that as a man has a brain on both sides, he should have a heart on both sides. Yet scientific men are still organizing expeditions to find the North Pole, because they are so fond of flat country. Scientific men are also still organizing expeditions to find a man's heart; and when they try to find it, they generally get on the wrong side of him.

Now, actual insight or inspiration is best tested by whether it guesses these hidden malformations or surprises. If our mathematician from the moon saw the two arms and the two ears, he might deduce the two shoulder-blades and the two halves of the brain. But if he guessed that the man's heart was in the right place, then I should call him something more than a mathematician. Now, this is exactly the claim which I have since come to propound for Christianity. Not merely that it deduces logical truths, but that when it suddenly becomes illogical, it has found, so to speak, an illogical truth. It not only goes right about things, but it goes wrong (if one may say so) exactly where the things go wrong. Its plan suits the secret irregularities, and expects the unexpected. It is simple about the simple truth; but it is stubborn about the subtle truth. It will admit that a man has two hands, it will not admit (though all the Modernists wail to it) the obvious deduction that he has two hearts. It is my only purpose in this chapter to point this out; to show that whenever we feel there is something odd in Christian theology, we shall generally find that there is something odd in the truth.

I have alluded to an unmeaning phrase to the effect that such and such a creed cannot be believed in our age. Of course, anything can be believed in any age. But, oddly enough, there really is a sense in which a creed, if it is believed at all, can be believed more fixedly in a complex society than in a simple one. If a man finds Christianity true in Birmingham, he has actually clearer reasons for faith than if he had found it true in Mercia. For the more complicated seems the coincidence, the less it can be a coincidence. If snowflakes fell in the shape, say, of the heart of Midlothian, it might be an accident. But if snowflakes fell in the exact shape of the maze at Hampton Court, I think one might call it a miracle. It is exactly as of such a miracle that I have since come to feel of the philosophy of Christianity. The complication of our modern world proves the truth of the creed more perfectly than any of the plain problems of the ages of faith. It was in Notting Hill and Battersea that I began to see that Christianity was true. This is why the faith has that elaboration of doctrines and details which so much distresses those who admire Christianity without believing in it. When once one believes in a creed, one is proud of its complexity, as scientists are proud of the complexity of science. It shows how rich it is in discoveries. If it is right at all, it is a compliment to say that it's elaborately right. A stick might fit a hole or a stone a hollow by accident. But a key and a lock are both complex. And if a key fits a lock, you know it is the right key.

But this involved accuracy of the thing makes it very difficult to do what I now have to do, to describe this accumulation of truth. It is very hard for a man to defend anything of which he is entirely convinced. It is comparatively easy when he is only partially convinced. He is partially convinced because he has found this or that proof of the thing, and he can expound it. But a man is not really convinced of a philosophic theory when he finds that something proves it. He is only really convinced when he finds that everything proves it. And the more converging reasons he finds pointing to this conviction, the more bewildered he is if asked suddenly to sum them up. Thus, if one asked an ordinary intelligent man, on the spur of the moment, "Why do you prefer civilization to savagery?" he would look wildly round at object after object, and would only be able to answer vaguely, "Why, there is that bookcase . . . and the coals in the coal-scuttle . . . and pianos . . . and policemen." The whole case for civilization is that the case for it is complex. It has done so many things. But that very multiplicity of proof which ought to make reply overwhelming makes reply impossible.

There is, therefore, about all complete conviction a

kind of huge helplessness. The belief is so big that it takes a long time to get it into action. And this hesitation chiefly arises, oddly enough, from an indifference about where one should begin. All roads lead to Rome; which is one reason why many people never get there. In the case of this defence of the Christian conviction I confess that I would as soon begin the argument with one thing as another; I would begin it with a turnip or a taximeter cab. But if I am to be at all careful about making my meaning clear, it will, I think, be wiser to continue the current arguments of the last chapter, which was concerned to urge the first of these mystical coincidences, or rather ratifications. All I had hitherto heard of Christian theology had alienated me from it. I was a pagan at the age of twelve, and a complete agnostic by the age of sixteen; and I cannot understand any one passing the age of seventeen without having asked himself so simple a question. I did, indeed, retain a cloudy reverence for a cosmic deity and a great historical interest in the Founder of Christianity. But I certainly regarded Him as a man; though perhaps I thought that, even in that point, He had an advantage over some of His modern critics. I read the scientific and sceptical literature of my time—all of it, at least, that I could find written in English and lying about; and I read nothing else; I mean I read nothing else on any other note of philosophy. The penny dreadfuls which I also read were indeed in a healthy and heroic tradition of Christianity; but I did not know this at the time. I never read a line of Christian apologetics. I read as little as I can of them now. It was Huxley and Herbert Spencer and Bradlaugh who brought me back to orthodox theology. They sowed in my mind my first wild doubts of doubt. Our grandmothers were quite right when they said that Tom Paine and the free-thinkers unsettled the mind. They do. They unsettled mine horribly. The rationalist made me question whether reason was of any use whatever; and when I had finished Herbert Spencer I had got as far as doubting (for the first time) whether evolution had occurred at all. As I laid down the last of Colonel Ingersoll's atheistic lectures the dreadful thought broke across my mind, "Almost thou persuadest me to be a Christian." I was in a desperate way.

This odd effect of the great agnostics in arousing doubts deeper than their own might be illustrated in many ways. I take only one. As I read and re-read all the non-Christian or anti-Christian accounts of the faith, from Huxley to Bradlaugh, a slow and awful impression grew gradually but graphically upon my mind—the impression that Christianity must be a most extraordinary thing. For not only (as I understood) had Christianity the most flaming vices, but it had apparently a mystical talent for combining vices which seemed inconsistent with each other. It was attacked on all sides and for all contradictory reasons. No sooner had one rationalist demonstrated that it was too far to the east than another demonstrated with equal clearness that it was much too far to the west. No sooner had my indignation died down at its angular and aggressive squareness than I was called up again to notice and condemn its enervating and sensual roundness. In case any reader has not come across the thing I mean, I will give such instances as I remember at random of this self-contradiction in the sceptical attack. I give four or five of them; there are fifty more.

Thus, for instance, I was much moved by the eloquent attack on Christianity as a thing of inhuman gloom; for I thought (and still think) sincere pessimism the unpardonable sin. Insincere pessimism is a social accomplishment, rather agreeable than otherwise; and fortunately nearly all pessimism is insincere. But if Christianity was, as these people said, a thing purely pessimistic and opposed to life, then I was quite prepared to blow up St. Paul's Cathedral. But the extraordinary thing is this. They did prove to me in Chapter I. (to my complete satisfaction) that Christianity was too pessimistic; and then, in Chapter II., they began to prove to me that it was a great deal too optimistic. One accusation against Christianity was that it prevented men, by morbid tears and terrors, from seeking joy and liberty in the bosom of Nature. But another accusation was that it comforted men with a fictitious providence, and put them in a pink-and-white nursery. One great agnostic asked why Nature was not beautiful enough, and why it was hard to be free. Another great agnostic objected that Christian optimism, "the garment of make-believe woven by pious hands," hid from us the fact that Nature was ugly, and that it was impossible to be free. One rationalist had hardly done calling Christianity a nightmare before another began to call it a fool's paradise. This puzzled me; the charges seemed inconsistent. Christianity could not at once be the black mask on a white world, and also the white mask on a black world. The state of the Christian could not be at once so comfortable that he was a coward to cling to it, and so uncomfortable that he was a fool to stand it. If it falsified human vision it must falsify it one way or another; it could not wear both green and rose-coloured spectacles. I rolled on my tongue with a terrible joy, as did all young men of that time, the taunts which Swinburne hurled at the dreariness of the creed—

"Thou hast conquered, O pale Galilean, the world
   has grown gray with Thy breath."

But when I read the same poet's accounts of paganism (as in "Atalanta"), I gathered that the world was, if possible, more gray before the Galilean breathed on it than afterwards. The poet maintained, indeed, in the abstract, that life itself was pitch dark. And yet, somehow, Christianity had darkened it. The very man who denounced Christianity for pessimism was himself a pessimist. I thought there must be something wrong. And it did for one wild moment cross my mind that, perhaps, those might not be the very best judges of the relation of religion to happiness who, by their own account, had neither one nor the other.

It must be understood that I did not conclude hastily that the accusations were false or the accusers fools. I simply deduced that Christianity must be something even weirder and wickeder than they made out. A thing might have these two opposite vices; but it must be a rather queer thing if it did. A man might be too fat in one place and too thin in another; but he would be an odd shape. At this point my thoughts were only of the odd shape of the Christian religion; I did not allege any odd shape in the rationalistic mind.

Here is another case of the same kind. I felt that a strong case against Christianity lay in the charge that there is something timid, monkish, and unmanly about all that is called "Christian," especially in its attitude towards resistance and fighting. The great sceptics of the nineteenth century were largely virile. Bradlaugh in an expansive way, Huxley, in a reticent way, were decidedly men. In comparison, it did seem tenable that there was something weak and over patient about Christian counsels. The Gospel paradox about the other cheek, the fact that priests never fought, a hundred things made plausible the accusation that Christianity was an attempt to make a man too like a sheep. I read it and believed it, and if I had read nothing different, I should have gone on believing it. But I read something very different. I turned the next page in my agnostic manual, and my brain turned up-side down. Now I found that I was to hate Christianity not for fighting too little, but for fighting too much. Christianity, it seemed, was the mother of wars. Christianity had deluged the world with blood. I had got thoroughly angry with the Christian, because he never was angry. And now I was told to be angry with him because his anger had been the most huge and horrible thing in human history; because his anger had soaked the earth and smoked to the sun. The very people who reproached Christianity with the meekness and non-resistance of the monasteries were the very people who reproached it also with the violence and valour of the Crusades. It was the fault of poor old Christianity (somehow or other) both that Edward the Confessor did not fight and that Richard Coeur de Leon did. The Quakers (we were told) were the only characteristic Christians; and yet the massacres of Cromwell and Alva were characteristic Christian crimes. What could it all mean? What was this Christianity which always forbade war and always produced wars? What could be the nature of the thing which one could abuse first because it would not fight, and second because it was always fighting? In what world of riddles was born this monstrous murder and this monstrous meekness? The shape of Christianity grew a queerer shape every instant.

I take a third case; the strangest of all, because it involves the one real objection to the faith. The one real objection to the Christian religion is simply that it is one religion. The world is a big place, full of very different kinds of people. Christianity (it may reasonably be said) is one thing confined to one kind of people; it began in Palestine, it has practically stopped with Europe. I was duly impressed with this argument in my youth, and I was much drawn towards the doctrine often preached in Ethical Societies—I mean the doctrine that there is one great unconscious church of all humanity founded on the omnipresence of the human conscience. Creeds, it was said, divided men; but at least morals united them. The soul might seek the strangest and most remote lands and ages and still find essential ethical common sense. It might find Confucius under Eastern trees, and he would be writing "Thou shalt not steal." It might decipher the darkest hieroglyphic on the most primeval desert, and the meaning when deciphered would be "Little boys should tell the truth." I believed this doctrine of the brotherhood of all men in the possession of a moral sense, and I believe it still—with other things. And I was thoroughly annoyed with Christianity for suggesting (as I supposed) that whole ages and empires of men had utterly escaped this light of justice and reason. But then I found an astonishing thing. I found that the very people who said that mankind was one church from Plato to Emerson were the very people who said that morality had changed altogether, and that what was right in one age was wrong in another. If I asked, say, for an altar, I was told that we needed none, for men our brothers gave us clear oracles and one creed in their universal customs and ideals. But if I mildly pointed out that one of men's universal customs was to have an altar, then my agnostic teachers turned clean round and told me that men had always been in darkness and the superstitions of savages. I found it was their daily taunt against Christianity that it was the light of one people and had left all others to die in the dark. But I also found that it was their special boast for themselves that science and progress were the discovery of one people, and that all other peoples had died in the dark. Their chief insult to Christianity was actually their chief compliment to themselves, and there seemed to be a strange unfairness about all their relative insistence on the two things. When considering some pagan or agnostic, we were to remember that all men had one religion; when considering some mystic or spiritualist, we were only to consider what absurd religions some men had. We could trust the ethics of Epictetus, because ethics had never changed. We must not trust the ethics of Bossuet, because ethics had changed. They changed in two hundred years, but not in two thousand.

This began to be alarming. It looked not so much as if Christianity was bad enough to include any vices, but rather as if any stick was good enough to beat Christianity with. What again could this astonishing thing be like which people were so anxious to contradict, that in doing so they did not mind contradicting themselves? I saw the same thing on every side. I can give no further space to this discussion of it in detail; but lest any one supposes that I have unfairly selected three accidental cases I will run briefly through a few others. Thus, certain sceptics wrote that the great crime of Christianity had been its attack on the family; it had dragged women to the loneliness and contemplation of the cloister, away from their homes and their children. But, then, other sceptics (slightly more advanced) said that the great crime of Christianity was forcing the family and marriage upon us; that it doomed women to the drudgery of their homes and children, and forbade them loneliness and contemplation. The charge was actually reversed. Or, again, certain phrases in the Epistles or the marriage service, were said by the anti-Christians to show contempt for woman's intellect. But I found that the anti-Christians themselves had a contempt for woman's intellect; for it was their great sneer at the Church on the Continent that "only women" went to it. Or again, Christianity was reproached with its naked and hungry habits; with its sackcloth and dried peas. But the next minute Christianity was being reproached with its pomp and its ritualism; its shrines of porphyry and its robes of gold. It was abused for being too plain and for being too coloured. Again Christianity had always been accused of restraining sexuality too much, when Bradlaugh the Malthusian discovered that it restrained it too little. It is often accused in the same breath of prim respectability and of religious extravagance. Between the covers of the same atheistic pamphlet I have found the faith rebuked for its disunion, "One thinks one thing, and one another," and rebuked also for its union, "It is difference of opinion that prevents the world from going to the dogs." In the same conversation a free-thinker, a friend of mine, blamed Christianity for despising Jews, and then despised it himself for being Jewish.

I wished to be quite fair then, and I wish to be quite fair now; and I did not conclude that the attack on Christianity was all wrong. I only concluded that if Christianity was wrong, it was very wrong indeed. Such hostile horrors might be combined in one thing, but that thing must be very strange and solitary. There are men who are misers, and also spendthrifts; but they are rare. There are men sensual and also ascetic; but they are rare. But if this mass of mad contradictions really existed, quakerish and blood-thirsty, too gorgeous and too thread-bare, austere, yet pandering preposterously to the lust of the eye, the enemy of women and their foolish refuge, a solemn pessimist and a silly optimist, if this evil existed, then there was in this evil something quite supreme and unique. For I found in my rationalist teachers no explanation of such exceptional corruption. Christianity (theoretically speaking) was in their eyes only one of the ordinary myths and errors of mortals. *They* gave me no key to this twisted and unnatural badness. Such a paradox of evil rose to the stature of the supernatural. It was, indeed, almost as supernatural as the infallibility of the Pope. An historic institution, which never went right, is really quite as much of a miracle as an institution that cannot go wrong. The only explanation which immediately occurred to my mind was that Christianity did not come from heaven, but from hell. Really, if Jesus of Nazareth was not Christ, He must have been Antichrist.

And then in a quiet hour a strange thought struck me like a still thunderbolt. There had suddenly come into my mind another explanation. Suppose we heard an unknown man spoken of by many men. Suppose we were puzzled to hear that some men said he was too tall and some too short; some objected to his fatness, some lamented his lean- ness; some thought him too dark, and some too fair. One explanation (as has been already admitted) would be that he might be an odd shape. But there is another explanation. He might be the right shape. Outrageously tall men might feel him to be short. Very short men might feel him to be tall. Old bucks who are growing stout might consider him insufficiently filled out; old beaux who were growing thin might feel that he expanded beyond the narrow lines of ele- gance. Perhaps Swedes (who have pale hair like tow) called him a dark man, while negroes considered him distinctly blonde. Perhaps (in short) this extraordinary thing is really the ordinary thing; at least the normal thing, the centre. Perhaps, after all, it is Christianity that is sane and all its critics that are mad—in various ways. I tested this idea by asking myself whether there was about any of the accusers anything morbid that might explain the accusation. I was startled to find that this key fitted a lock. For instance, it was certainly odd that the modern world charged Christianity at once with bodily austerity and with artistic pomp. But then it was also odd, very odd, that the modern world itself combined extreme bodily luxury with an extreme absence of artistic pomp. The modern man thought Becket's robes too rich and his meals too poor. But then the modern man was really exceptional in history; no man before ever ate such elaborate dinners in such ugly clothes. The modern man found the church too simple exactly where modern life is too complex; he found the church too gorgeous exactly where modern life is too dingy. The man who disliked the plain fasts and feasts was mad on entrées. The man who disliked vestments wore a pair of preposterous trousers. And surely if there was any insanity involved in the matter at all it was in the trousers, not in the simply falling robe. If there was any insanity at all, it was in the extravagant entrées, not in the bread and wine.

I went over all the cases, and I found the key fitted so far. The fact that Swinburne was irritated at the unhappiness of Christians and yet more irritated at their happiness was easily explained. It was no longer a complication of diseases in Christianity, but a complication of diseases in Swinburne. The restraints of Christians saddened him simply because he was more hedonist than a healthy man should be. The faith of Christians angered him because he was more pessimist than a healthy man should be. In the same way the Malthusians by instinct attacked Christianity; not because there is anything especially anti-Malthusian about Christianity, but because there is something a little anti-human about Malthusianism.

Nevertheless it could not, I felt, be quite true that Christianity was merely sensible and stood in the middle. There was really an element in it of emphasis and even frenzy which had justified the secularists in their superficial criticism. It might be wise, I began more and more to think that it was wise, but it was not merely worldly wise; it was not merely temperate and respectable. Its fierce crusaders and meek saints might balance each other; still, the crusaders were very fierce and the saints were very meek, meek beyond all decency. Now, it was just at this point of the speculation that I remembered my thoughts about the martyr and the suicide. In that matter there had been this combination between two almost insane positions which yet somehow amounted to sanity. This was just such another contradiction; and this I had already found to be true. This was exactly one of the paradoxes in which sceptics found the creed wrong; and in this I had found it right. Madly as Christians might love the martyr or hate the suicide, they never felt these passions more madly than I had felt them long before I dreamed of Christianity. Then the most difficult and interesting part of the mental process opened, and I began to trace this idea darkly through all the enormous thoughts of our theology. The idea was that which I had outlined touching the optimist and the pessimist; that we want not an amalgam or compromise, but both things at the top of their energy; love and wrath both burning. Here I shall only trace it in relation to ethics. But I need not remind the reader that the idea of this combination is indeed central in orthodox theology. For orthodox theology has specially insisted that Christ was not a being apart from God and man, like an elf, nor yet a being half human and half not, like a centaur, but both things at once and both things thoroughly, very man and very God. Now let me trace this notion as I found it.

All sane men can see that sanity is some kind of equilibrium; that one may be mad and eat too much, or mad and eat too little. Some moderns have indeed appeared with vague versions of progress and evolution which seeks to destroy the *meson* or balance of Aristotle. They seem to suggest that we are meant to starve progressively, or to go on eating larger and larger breakfasts every morning for ever. But the great truism of the *meson* remains for all thinking men, and these people have not upset any balance except their own. But granted that we have all to keep a balance, the real interest comes in with the question of how that balance can be kept. That was the problem which Paganism tried to solve: that was the problem which I think Christianity solved and solved in a very strange way.

Paganism declared that virtue was in a balance; Christianity declared it was in a conflict: the collision of two passions apparently opposite. Of course they were not really inconsistent; but they were such that it was hard to hold simultaneously. Let us follow for a moment the clue of the martyr and the suicide; and take the case of courage. No quality has ever so much addled the brains and tangled the definitions of merely rational sages. Courage is almost a contradiction in terms. It means a strong desire to live taking the form of a readiness to die. "He that will lose his life, the same shall save it," is not a piece of mysticism for saints and heroes. It is a piece of everyday advice for sailors or mountaineers. It might be printed in an Alpine guide or a drill book. This paradox is the whole principle of courage; even of quite earthly or quite brutal courage. A man cut off by the sea may save his life if he will risk it on the precipice.

He can only get away from death by continually stepping within an inch of it. A soldier surrounded by enemies, if he is to cut his way out, needs to combine a strong desire for living with a strange carelessness about dying. He must not merely cling to life, for then he will be a coward, and will not escape. He must not merely wait for death, for then he will be a suicide, and will not escape. He must seek his life in a spirit of furious indifference to it; he must desire life like water and yet drink death like wine. No philosopher, I fancy, has ever expressed this romantic riddle with adequate lucidity, and I certainly have not done so. But Christianity has done more: it has marked the limits of it in the awful graves of the suicide and the hero, showing the distance between him who dies for the sake of living and him who dies for the sake of dying. And it has held up ever since above the European lances the banner of the mystery of chivalry: the Christian courage, which is a disdain of death; not the Chinese courage, which is a disdain of life.

And now I began to find that this duplex passion was the Christian key to ethics everywhere. Everywhere the creed made a moderation out of the still crash of two impetuous emotions. Take, for instance, the matter of modesty, of the balance between mere pride and mere prostration. The average pagan, like the average agnostic, would merely say that he was content with himself, but not insolently self-satisfied, that there were many better and many worse, that his deserts were limited, but he would see that he got them. In short, he would walk with his head in the air; but not necessarily with his nose in the air. This is a manly and rational position, but it is open to the objection we noted against the compromise between optimism and pessimism—the "resignation" of Matthew Arnold. Being a mixture of two things, it is a dilution of two things; neither is present in its full strength or contributes its full colour. This proper pride does not lift the heart like the tongue of trumpets; you cannot go clad in crimson and gold for this. On the other hand, this mild rationalist modesty does not cleanse the soul with fire and make it clear like crystal; it does not (like a strict and searching humility) make a man as a little child, who can sit at the feet of the grass. It does not make him look up and see marvels; for Alice must grow small if she is to be Alice in Wonderland. Thus it loses both the poetry of being proud and the poetry of being humble. Christianity sought by this same strange expedient to save both of them.

It separated the two ideas and then exaggerated them both. In one way Man was to be haughtier than he had ever been before; in another way he was to be humbler than he had ever been before. In so far as I am Man I am the chief of creatures. In so far as I am a man I am the chief of sinners. All humility that had meant pessimism, that had meant man taking a vague or mean view of his whole destiny—all that was to go. We were to hear no more the wail of Ecclesiastes that humanity had no pre-eminence over the brute, or the awful cry of Homer that man was only the saddest of all the beasts of the field. Man was a statue of God walking about the garden. Man had pre-eminence over all the brutes; man was only sad because he was not a beast, but a broken god. The Greek had spoken of men creeping on the earth, as if clinging to it. Now Man was to tread on the earth as if to subdue it. Christianity thus held a thought of the dignity of man that could only be expressed in crowns rayed like the sun and fans of peacock plumage. Yet at the same time it could hold a thought about the abject smallness of man that could only be expressed in fasting and fantastic submission, in the gray ashes of St. Dominic and the white snows of St. Bernard. When one came to think of *one's self*, there was vista and void enough for any amount of bleak abnegation and bitter truth. There the realistic gentleman could let himself go—as long as he let himself go at himself. There was an open playground for the happy pessimist. Let him say anything against himself short of blaspheming the original aim of his being; let him call himself a fool and even a damned fool (though that is Calvinistic); but he must not say that fools are not worth saving. He must not say that a man, *qua* man, can be valueless. Here, again in short, Christianity got over the difficulty of combining furious opposites, by keeping them both, and keeping them both furious. The Church was positive on both points. One can hardly think too little of one's self. One can hardly think too much of one's soul.

Take another case: the complicated question of charity, which some highly uncharitable idealists seem to think quite easy. Charity is a paradox, like modesty and courage. Stated baldly, charity certainly means one of two things— pardoning unpardonable acts, or loving unlovable people. But if we ask ourselves (as we did in the case of pride) what a sensible pagan would feel about such a subject, we shall probably be beginning at the bottom of it. A sensible pagan would say that there were some people one could forgive, and some one couldn't: a slave who stole wine could be laughed at; a slave who betrayed his benefactor could be killed, and cursed even after he was killed. In so far as the act was pardonable, the man was pardonable. That again is rational, and even refreshing; but it is a dilution. It leaves no place for a pure horror of injustice, such as that which is a great beauty in the innocent. And it leaves no place for a mere tenderness for men as men, such as is the whole fascination of the charitable. Christianity came in here as before. It came in startlingly with a sword, and clove one thing from another. It divided the crime from the criminal. The criminal we must forgive unto seventy times seven. The crime we must not forgive at all. It was not enough that slaves who stole wine inspired partly anger and partly kindness. We must be much more angry with theft than before, and yet much kinder to thieves than before. There was room for wrath and love to run wild. And the more I considered Christianity, the more I found that while it had established a rule and order, the chief aim of that order was to give room for good things to run wild.

Mental and emotional liberty are not so simple as they look. Really they require almost as careful a balance of laws and conditions as do social and political liberty. The ordinary aesthetic anarchist who sets out to feel everything freely gets knotted at last in a paradox that prevents him feeling at all. He breaks away from home limits to follow poetry. But in ceasing to feel home limits he has ceased to feel the "Odyssey." He is free from national prejudices and outside patriotism. But being outside patriotism he is outside "Henry V." Such a literary man is simply outside all literature: he is more of a prisoner than any bigot. For if there is a wall between you and the world, it makes little difference whether you describe yourself as locked in or as locked out. What we want is not the universality that is outside all normal sentiments; we want the universality that is inside all normal sentiments. It is all the difference between being free from them, as a man is free from a prison, and being free of them as a man is free of a city. I am free from Windsor Castle (that is, I am not forcibly detained there), but I am by no means free of that building. How can man be approximately free of fine emotions, able to swing them in a clear space without breakage or wrong? *This* was the achievement of this Christian paradox of the parallel passions. Granted the primary dogma of the war between divine and diabolic, the revolt and ruin of the world, their optimism and pessimism, as pure poetry, could be loosened like cataracts.

St. Francis, in praising all good, could be a more shouting optimist than Walt Whitman. St. Jerome, in denouncing all evil, could paint the world blacker than Schopenhauer. Both passions were free because both were kept in their place. The optimist could pour out all the praise he liked on the gay music of the march, the golden trumpets, and the purple banners going into battle. But he must not call the fight needless. The pessimist might draw as darkly as he chose the sickening marches or the sanguine wounds. But he must not call the fight hopeless. So it was with all the other moral problems, with pride, with protest, and with compassion. By defining its main doctrine, the Church not only kept seemingly inconsistent things side by side, but, what was more, allowed them to break out in a sort of artistic violence otherwise possible only to anarchists. Meekness grew more dramatic than madness. Historic Christianity rose into a high and strange *coup de théâtre* of morality—things that are to virtue what the crimes of Nero are to vice. The spirits of indignation and of charity took terrible and attractive forms, ranging from that monkish fierceness that scourged like a dog the first and greatest of the Plantagenets, to the sublime pity of St. Catherine, who, in the official shambles, kissed the bloody head of the criminal. Poetry could be acted as well as composed. This heroic and monumental manner in ethics has entirely vanished with supernatural religion. They, being humble, could parade themselves: but we are too proud to be prominent. Our ethical teachers write reasonably for prison reform; but we are not likely to see Mr. Cadbury, or any eminent philanthropist, go into Reading Gaol and embrace the strangled corpse before it is cast into the quicklime. Our ethical teachers write mildly against the power of millionaires; but we are not likely to see Mr. Rockefeller, or any modern tyrant, publicly whipped in Westminster Abbey.

Thus, the double charges of the secularists, though throwing nothing but darkness and confusion on themselves, throw a real light on the faith. It is true that the historic Church has at once emphasised celibacy and emphasised the family; has at once (if one may put it so) been fiercely for having children and fiercely for not having children. It has kept them side by side like two strong colours, red and white, like the red and white upon the shield of St. George. It has always had a healthy hatred of pink. It hates that combination of two colours which is the feeble expedient of the philosophers. It hates that evolution of black into white which is tantamount to a dirty gray. In fact, the whole theory of the Church on virginity might be symbolized in the statement that white is a colour: not merely the absence of a colour. All that I am urging here can be expressed by saying that Christianity sought in most of these cases to keep two colours coexistent but pure. It is not a mixture like russet or purple; it is rather like a shot silk, for a shot silk is always at right angles, and is in the pattern of the cross.

So it is also, of course, with the contradictory charges of the anti-Christians about submission and slaughter. It *is* true that the Church told some men to fight and others not to fight; and it *is* true that those who fought were like thunderbolts and those who did not fight were like statues. All this simply means that the Church preferred to use its Supermen and to use its Tolstoyans. There must be *some* good in the life of battle, for so many good men have enjoyed being soldiers. There must be *some* good in the idea of non-resistance, for so many good men seem to enjoy being Quakers. All that the Church did (so far as that goes) was to prevent either of these good things from ousting the other. They existed side by side. The Tolstoyans, having all the scruples of monks, simply became monks. The Quakers became a club instead of becoming a sect. Monks said all that Tolstoy says; they poured out lucid lamentations about the cruelty of battles and the vanity of revenge. But the Tolstoyans are not quite right enough to run the whole world; and in the ages of faith they were not allowed to run it. The world did not lose the last charge of Sir James Douglas or the banner of Joan the Maid. And sometimes this pure gentleness and this pure fierceness met and justified their juncture; the paradox of all the prophets was fulfilled, and, in the soul of St. Louis, the lion lay down with the lamb. But remember that this text is too lightly interpreted. It is constantly assured, especially in our Tolstoyan tendencies, that when the lion lies down with the lamb the lion becomes lamb-like. But that is brutal annexation and imperialism on the part of the lamb. That is simply the lamb absorbing the lion instead of the lion eating the lamb. The real problem is—Can the lion lie down with the lamb and still retain his royal ferocity? *That* is the problem the Church attempted; *that* is the miracle she achieved.

This is what I have called guessing the hidden eccentricities of life. This is knowing that a man's heart is to the left and not in the middle. This is knowing not only that the earth is round, but knowing exactly where it is flat. Christian doctrine detected the oddities of life. It not only discovered the law, but it foresaw the exceptions. Those underrate Christianity who say that it discovered mercy; any one might discover mercy. In fact every one did. But to discover a plan for being merciful and also severe—*that* was to anticipate a strange need of human nature. For no one wants to be forgiven for a big sin as if it were a little one. Any one might say that we should be neither quite miserable nor quite happy. But to find out how far one *may* be quite miserable without making it impossible to be quite happy—that was a discovery in psychology. Any one might say, "Neither swagger nor grovel"; and it would have been a limit. But to say, "Here you can swagger and there you can grovel"—that was an emancipation.

This was the big fact about Christian ethics; the discovery of the new balance. Paganism had been like a pillar of marble, upright because proportioned with symmetry. Christianity was like a huge and ragged and romantic rock, which, though it sways on its pedestal at a touch, yet, because its exaggerated excrescences exactly balance each other, is enthroned there for a thousand years. In a Gothic cathedral the columns were all different, but they were all necessary. Every support seemed an accidental and fantastic support; every buttress was a flying buttress. So in Christendom apparent accidents balanced. Becket wore a hair shirt under his gold and crimson, and there is much to be said for the combination; for Becket got the benefit of the hair shirt while the people in the street got the benefit of the crimson and gold. It is at least better than the manner of the modern millionaire, who has the black and the drab outwardly for others, and the gold next his heart. But the balance was not always in one man's body as in Becket's; the balance was often distributed over the whole body of Christendom. Because a man prayed and fasted on the Northern snows, flowers could be flung at his festival in the Southern cities; and because fanatics drank water on the sands of Syria, men could still drink cider in the orchards of England. This is what makes Christendom at once so much more perplexing and so much more interesting than the Pagan empire; just as Amiens Cathedral is not better but more interesting than the Parthenon. If any one wants a modern proof of all this, let him consider the curious fact that, under Christianity, Europe (while remaining a unity) has broken up into individual nations. Patriotism is a perfect example of this deliberate balancing of one emphasis against another emphasis. The instinct of the Pagan empire would have said, "You shall all be Roman citizens, and grow alike; let the German grow less slow and reverent; the Frenchmen less experimental and swift." But the instinct of Christian Europe says, "Let the German remain slow and reverent, that the Frenchman may the more safely be swift and experimental. We will make an equipoise out of these excesses. The absurdity called Germany shall correct the insanity called France."

Last and most important, it is exactly this which explains what is so inexplicable to all the modern critics of the history of Christianity. I mean the monstrous wars about small points of theology, the earthquakes of emotion about a gesture or a word. It was only a matter of an inch; but an inch is everything when you are balancing. The Church could not afford to swerve a hair's breadth on some things if she was to continue her great and daring experiment of the irregular equilibrium. Once let one idea become less powerful and some other idea would become too powerful. It was no flock of sheep the Christian shepherd was leading, but a herd of bulls and tigers, of terrible ideals and devouring doctrines, each one of them strong enough to turn to a false religion and lay waste the world. Remember that the Church went in specifically for dangerous ideas; she was a lion tamer. The idea of birth through a Holy Spirit, of the death of a divine being, of the forgiveness of sins, or the fulfilment of prophecies, are ideas which, any one can see, need but a touch to turn them into something blasphemous or ferocious. The smallest link was let drop by the artificers of the Mediterranean, and the lion of ancestral pessimism burst his chain in the forgotten forests of the north. Of these theological equalisations I have to speak afterwards. Here it is enough to notice that if some small mistake were made in doctrine, huge blunders might be made in human happiness. A sentence phrased wrong about the nature of symbolism would have broken all the best statues in Europe. A slip in the definitions might stop all the dances; might wither all the Christmas trees or break all the Easter eggs. Doctrines had to be defined within strict limits, even in order that man might enjoy general human liberties. The Church had to be careful, if only that the world might be careless.

This is the thrilling romance of Orthodoxy. People have fallen into a foolish habit of speaking of orthodoxy as something heavy, humdrum, and safe. There never was anything so perilous or so exciting as orthodoxy. It was sanity: and to be sane is more dramatic than to be mad. It was the equilibrium of a man behind madly rushing horses, seeming to stoop this way and to sway that, yet in every attitude having the grace of statuary and the accuracy of arithmetic. The Church in its early days went fierce and fast with any war-horse; yet it is utterly unhistoric to say that she merely went mad along one idea, like a vulgar fanaticism. She swerved to left and right, so exactly as to avoid enormous obstacles. She left on one hand the huge bulk of Arianism, buttressed by all the worldly powers to make Christianity too worldly. The next instant she was swerving to avoid an orientalism, which would have made it too unworldly. The orthodox Church never took the tame course or accepted the conventions; the orthodox Church was never respectable. It would have been easier to have accepted the earthly power of the Arians. It would have been easy, in the Calvinistic seventeenth century, to fall into the bottomless pit of predestination. It is easy to be a madman: it is easy to be a heretic. It is always easy to let the age have its head; the difficult thing is to keep one's own. It is always easy to be a modernist; as it is easy to be a snob. To have fallen into any of those open traps of error and exaggeration which fashion after fashion and sect after sect set along the historic path of Christendom—that would indeed have been simple. It is always simple to fall; there are an infinity of angles at which one falls, only one at which one stands. To have fallen into any one of the fads from Gnosticism to Christian Science would indeed have been obvious and tame. But to have avoided them all has been one whirling adventure; and in my vision the heavenly chariot flies thundering through the ages, the dull heresies sprawling and prostrate, the wild truth reeling but erect.

The Power of Paradox

1. On your own or in a small group, work together to find as many
   satisfying paradoxes as you can. The names of God and Jesus are a
   great start (e.g., Jesus is "the Lion of the tribe of Judah" [Revelation
   5:5] and "the Lamb of God who takes away the sin of the world"
   [John 1:29]). Jesus and Solomon utter a whole bunch as well
   (e.g., "If you cling to your life, you will lose it; but if you give up
   your life for me, you will find it" [Matthew 10:39]).

2. Take a moment to reflect on where you may have been trying to
   resolve the tensions of a paradox in your journey—to make life
   simpler and understandable at the expense of truth. Why is this
   approach tempting? Why is it ultimately unsatisfying?

3. Consider where you have not been choosing to live into the tension of a paradox. How could you take the step of trust and courage to repent and move closer to the truth found in the tension of paradox?

4. Examine this chart of biblical paradoxes, and fill in the blanks with other paradoxes you find in Scripture.

Lion		Lamb
Justice	T	Mercy
Simple	R	Complex
Fully God		Fully Man
Grace	U	Works
Free Will	T	God-ordained
_____	H	_____
_____		_____
_____		_____

Mere Christianity and Evidence for God

At this point in our worldview journey it is valuable to pick up a copy of C. S. Lewis's *Mere Christianity*.

I recommend that you read book 1, "Right and Wrong as a Clue to the Meaning of the Universe," with an open heart and mind. Lewis, without using any Bible verses or the name Jesus Christ, helps readers to follow a logical argument based on humanity's sense of morality down a clear-cut path toward a trustworthy conclusion that an objective, all-powerful, and benevolent God exists as our standard for morality. He also helps the reader understand that in order to have any real sense of morality, this type of personal God necessarily must exist. Lewis's words help us move through the sea of moral relativity found in materialism and monism, and they also help us move past objective morality as simply a concept as found in idealism into objective morality represented in a living being and given by a living being to humanity. Again, this is astounding because Lewis is able to accomplish this without directly quoting any passages in the Bible, which helps many people trust this process.

To extend your learning, for book 1, individually or in a small group or with your leader or mentor, create premises chapter by chapter for Lewis's logical argument that lead to the conclusion found in chapter 5 of book 1. There are some excellent "doodle" YouTube videos that recreate Lewis's original broadcast talks during World War II. These talks became the opening chapters of *Mere Christianity*. The doodles can help you follow Lewis's logical argument. You can find them on your own, or I've linked to them on IntheTrueMyth.org.

To further extend this learning adventure, read book 2 of *Mere Christianity*, "What Christians Believe." This next section helps the reader move from believing in God as a living and loving being into navigating why trusting in Jesus, not just "God," is an essential part of the worldview journey, especially for Christians. Again, I invite you to put aside denominational bias or even religious bias and to move from reading the Gospel of John, which you read at the end of part 2, into reading these pages from Lewis about why trusting in the Jesus as represented in the Gospel of John is not just an add-on but the center of the entire "Christ-centered" worldview. One reason these assignments on C. S. Lewis are in this book is that Lewis was a staunch atheist for more than fifteen years after dismissing Christianity as an adolescent.

For book 2 of *Mere Christianity*, grab a highlighter and a pen or pencil and annotate the text, panning for as much gold as you can find. Most students find the profound simplicity of *Mere Christianity* refreshing to read after the complexity, weight, and density of G. K. Chesterton's *Orthodoxy*.

EXTEND YOUR LEARNING: Create at least three Instagram posts that you could share with the world if you wanted to from book 2 of *Mere Christianity*. (These could be in contrast to the tweets you created earlier from "The Madman" by Nietzsche.)

EXTEND YOUR LEARNING: Find and watch *The Magic Never Ends: The Life and Work of C. S. Lewis*, a documentary about the life of C. S. Lewis produced by Duncan Entertainment and narrated by Ben Kingsley. Discuss with a partner how Lewis came to faith and how his faith journey can help you in your own.

Romans 1–8 and
Mere Christianity

ANALYZING THE TEXT

In one sitting, read and annotate the opening chapters of the apostle Paul's letter to the church at Rome. Pretend you are a member of the church. In the opening pages of *Mere Christianity*, where do you see connections to Lewis's argument for the existence of God? The connections you make can be subtle, overt, literary, historical, artistic, personal, or metaphoric.

Highlight or underline at least three verses that you find engaging, and be prepared to briefly explain why you picked those verses.

SPACE TO
WRITE OR
DOODLE

ROMANS 1–8

Chapter 1

This letter is from Paul, a slave of Christ Jesus, chosen by God to be an apostle and sent out to preach his Good News. ²God promised this Good News long ago through his prophets in the holy Scriptures. ³The Good News is about his Son. In his earthly life he was born into King David's family line, ⁴and he was shown to be the Son of

God when he was raised from the dead by the power of the Holy Spirit. He is Jesus Christ our Lord. ⁵Through Christ, God has given us the privilege and authority as apostles to tell Gentiles everywhere what God has done for them, so that they will believe and obey him, bringing glory to his name.

⁶And you are included among those Gentiles who have been called to belong to Jesus Christ. ⁷I am writing to all of you in Rome who are loved by God and are called to be his own holy people.

May God our Father and the Lord Jesus Christ give you grace and peace.

⁸Let me say first that I thank my God through Jesus Christ for all of you, because your faith in him is being talked about all over the world. ⁹God knows how often I pray for you. Day and night I bring you and your needs in prayer to God, whom I serve with all my heart by spreading the Good News about his Son.

¹⁰One of the things I always pray for is the opportunity, God willing, to come at last to see you. ¹¹For I long to visit you so I can bring you some spiritual gift that will help you grow strong in the Lord. ¹²When we get together, I want to encourage you in your faith, but I also want to be encouraged by yours.

¹³I want you to know, dear brothers and sisters, that I planned many times to visit you, but I was prevented until now. I want to work among you and see spiritual fruit, just as I have seen among other Gentiles. ¹⁴For I have a great sense of obligation to people in both the civilized world and the rest of the world, to the educated and uneducated alike. ¹⁵So I am eager to come to you in Rome, too, to preach the Good News.

¹⁶For I am not ashamed of this Good News about Christ. It is the power of God at work, saving everyone

who believes—the Jew first and also the Gentile. [17]This Good News tells us how God makes us right in his sight. This is accomplished from start to finish by faith. As the Scriptures say, "It is through faith that a righteous person has life."

[18]But God shows his anger from heaven against all sinful, wicked people who suppress the truth by their wickedness. [19]They know the truth about God because he has made it obvious to them. [20]For ever since the world was created, people have seen the earth and sky. Through everything God made, they can clearly see his invisible qualities—his eternal power and divine nature. So they have no excuse for not knowing God.

[21]Yes, they knew God, but they wouldn't worship him as God or even give him thanks. And they began to think up foolish ideas of what God was like. As a result, their minds became dark and confused. [22]Claiming to be wise, they instead became utter fools. [23]And instead of worshiping the glorious, ever-living God, they worshiped idols made to look like mere people and birds and animals and reptiles.

[24]So God abandoned them to do whatever shameful things their hearts desired. As a result, they did vile and degrading things with each other's bodies. [25]They traded the truth about God for a lie. So they worshiped and served the things God created instead of the Creator himself, who is worthy of eternal praise! Amen. [26]That is why God abandoned them to their shameful desires. Even the women turned against the natural way to have sex and instead indulged in sex with each other. [27]And the men, instead of having normal sexual relations with women, burned with lust for each other. Men did shameful things with other men, and as a result of this sin, they suffered within themselves the penalty they deserved.

[28]Since they thought it foolish to acknowledge God, he abandoned them to their foolish thinking and let them do things that should never be done. [29]Their lives became full of every kind of wickedness, sin, greed, hate, envy, murder, quarreling, deception, malicious behavior, and gossip. [30]They are backstabbers, haters of God, insolent, proud, and boastful. They invent new ways of sinning, and they disobey their parents. [31]They refuse to understand, break their promises, are heartless, and have no mercy. [32]They know God's justice requires that those who do these things deserve to die, yet they do them anyway. Worse yet, they encourage others to do them, too.

Chapter 2

You may think you can condemn such people, but you are just as bad, and you have no excuse! When you say they are wicked and should be punished, you are condemning yourself, for you who judge others do these very same things. [2]And we know that God, in his justice, will punish anyone who does such things. [3]Since you judge others for doing these things, why do you think you can avoid God's judgment when you do the same things? [4]Don't you see how wonderfully kind, tolerant, and patient God is with you? Does this mean nothing to you? Can't you see that his kindness is intended to turn you from your sin?

[5]But because you are stubborn and refuse to turn from your sin, you are storing up terrible punishment for yourself. For a day of anger is coming, when God's righteous judgment will be revealed. [6]He will judge everyone according to what they have done. [7]He will give eternal life to those who keep on doing good, seeking after the glory and honor and immortality that God offers. [8]But he will pour out his anger and wrath on those who live for themselves, who refuse to obey the truth and instead live

lives of wickedness. ⁹There will be trouble and calamity for everyone who keeps on doing what is evil—for the Jew first and also for the Gentile. ¹⁰But there will be glory and honor and peace from God for all who do good—for the Jew first and also for the Gentile. ¹¹For God does not show favoritism.

¹²When the Gentiles sin, they will be destroyed, even though they never had God's written law. And the Jews, who do have God's law, will be judged by that law when they fail to obey it. ¹³For merely listening to the law doesn't make us right with God. It is obeying the law that makes us right in his sight. ¹⁴Even Gentiles, who do not have God's written law, show that they know his law when they instinctively obey it, even without having heard it. ¹⁵They demonstrate that God's law is written in their hearts, for their own conscience and thoughts either accuse them or tell them they are doing right. ¹⁶And this is the message I proclaim—that the day is coming when God, through Christ Jesus, will judge everyone's secret life.

¹⁷You who call yourselves Jews are relying on God's law, and you boast about your special relationship with him. ¹⁸You know what he wants; you know what is right because you have been taught his law. ¹⁹You are convinced that you are a guide for the blind and a light for people who are lost in darkness. ²⁰You think you can instruct the ignorant and teach children the ways of God. For you are certain that God's law gives you complete knowledge and truth.

²¹Well then, if you teach others, why don't you teach yourself? You tell others not to steal, but do you steal? ²²You say it is wrong to commit adultery, but do you commit adultery? You condemn idolatry, but do you use items stolen from pagan temples? ²³You are so proud of knowing the law, but you dishonor God by breaking it. ²⁴No

wonder the Scriptures say, "The Gentiles blaspheme the name of God because of you."

²⁵The Jewish ceremony of circumcision has value only if you obey God's law. But if you don't obey God's law, you are no better off than an uncircumcised Gentile. ²⁶And if the Gentiles obey God's law, won't God declare them to be his own people? ²⁷In fact, uncircumcised Gentiles who keep God's law will condemn you Jews who are circumcised and possess God's law but don't obey it.

²⁸For you are not a true Jew just because you were born of Jewish parents or because you have gone through the ceremony of circumcision. ²⁹No, a true Jew is one whose heart is right with God. And true circumcision is not merely obeying the letter of the law; rather, it is a change of heart produced by the Spirit. And a person with a changed heart seeks praise from God, not from people.

Chapter 3

Then what's the advantage of being a Jew? Is there any value in the ceremony of circumcision? ²Yes, there are great benefits! First of all, the Jews were entrusted with the whole revelation of God.

³True, some of them were unfaithful; but just because they were unfaithful, does that mean God will be unfaithful? ⁴Of course not! Even if everyone else is a liar, God is true. As the Scriptures say about him,

"You will be proved right in what you say,
    and you will win your case in court."

⁵"But," some might say, "our sinfulness serves a good purpose, for it helps people see how righteous God is. Isn't it unfair, then, for him to punish us?" (This is merely a human point of view.) ⁶Of course not! If God were not

entirely fair, how would he be qualified to judge the world? [7]"But," someone might still argue, "how can God condemn me as a sinner if my dishonesty highlights his truthfulness and brings him more glory?" [8]And some people even slander us by claiming that we say, "The more we sin, the better it is!" Those who say such things deserve to be condemned.

[9]Well then, should we conclude that we Jews are better than others? No, not at all, for we have already shown that all people, whether Jews or Gentiles, are under the power of sin. [10]As the Scriptures say,

> "No one is righteous—
> not even one.
> [11]No one is truly wise;
> no one is seeking God.
> [12]All have turned away;
> all have become useless.
> No one does good,
> not a single one."
> [13]"Their talk is foul, like the stench from an
> open grave.
> Their tongues are filled with lies."
> "Snake venom drips from their lips."
> [14]"Their mouths are full of cursing and
> bitterness."
> [15]"They rush to commit murder.
> [16]Destruction and misery always follow them.
> [17]They don't know where to find peace."
> [18]"They have no fear of God at all."

[19]Obviously, the law applies to those to whom it was given, for its purpose is to keep people from having excuses, and to show that the entire world is guilty before God. [20]For no one can ever be made right with God by

doing what the law commands. The law simply shows us how sinful we are.

²¹But now God has shown us a way to be made right with him without keeping the requirements of the law, as was promised in the writings of Moses and the prophets long ago. ²²We are made right with God by placing our faith in Jesus Christ. And this is true for everyone who believes, no matter who we are.

²³For everyone has sinned; we all fall short of God's glorious standard. ²⁴Yet God, in his grace, freely makes us right in his sight. He did this through Christ Jesus when he freed us from the penalty for our sins. ²⁵For God presented Jesus as the sacrifice for sin. People are made right with God when they believe that Jesus sacrificed his life, shedding his blood. This sacrifice shows that God was being fair when he held back and did not punish those who sinned in times past, ²⁶for he was looking ahead and including them in what he would do in this present time. God did this to demonstrate his righteousness, for he himself is fair and just, and he makes sinners right in his sight when they believe in Jesus.

²⁷Can we boast, then, that we have done anything to be accepted by God? No, because our acquittal is not based on obeying the law. It is based on faith. ²⁸So we are made right with God through faith and not by obeying the law.

²⁹After all, is God the God of the Jews only? Isn't he also the God of the Gentiles? Of course he is. ³⁰There is only one God, and he makes people right with himself only by faith, whether they are Jews or Gentiles. ³¹Well then, if we emphasize faith, does this mean that we can forget about the law? Of course not! In fact, only when we have faith do we truly fulfill the law.

Chapter 4

Abraham was, humanly speaking, the founder of our Jewish nation. What did he discover about being made right with God? [2]If his good deeds had made him acceptable to God, he would have had something to boast about. But that was not God's way. [3]For the Scriptures tell us, "Abraham believed God, and God counted him as righteous because of his faith."

[4]When people work, their wages are not a gift, but something they have earned. [5]But people are counted as righteous, not because of their work, but because of their faith in God who forgives sinners. [6]David also spoke of this when he described the happiness of those who are declared righteous without working for it:

[7]"Oh, what joy for those
whose disobedience is forgiven,
whose sins are put out of sight.
[8]Yes, what joy for those
whose record the LORD has cleared of sin."

[9]Now, is this blessing only for the Jews, or is it also for uncircumcised Gentiles? Well, we have been saying that Abraham was counted as righteous by God because of his faith. [10]But how did this happen? Was he counted as righteous only after he was circumcised, or was it before he was circumcised? Clearly, God accepted Abraham before he was circumcised!

[11]Circumcision was a sign that Abraham already had faith and that God had already accepted him and declared him to be righteous—even before he was circumcised. So Abraham is the spiritual father of those who have faith but have not been circumcised. They are counted as righteous

because of their faith. [12]And Abraham is also the spiritual father of those who have been circumcised, but only if they have the same kind of faith Abraham had before he was circumcised.

[13]Clearly, God's promise to give the whole earth to Abraham and his descendants was based not on his obedience to God's law, but on a right relationship with God that comes by faith. [14]If God's promise is only for those who obey the law, then faith is not necessary and the promise is pointless. [15]For the law always brings punishment on those who try to obey it. (The only way to avoid breaking the law is to have no law to break!)

[16]So the promise is received by faith. It is given as a free gift. And we are all certain to receive it, whether or not we live according to the law of Moses, if we have faith like Abraham's. For Abraham is the father of all who believe. [17]That is what the Scriptures mean when God told him, "I have made you the father of many nations." This happened because Abraham believed in the God who brings the dead back to life and who creates new things out of nothing.

[18]Even when there was no reason for hope, Abraham kept hoping—believing that he would become the father of many nations. For God had said to him, "That's how many descendants you will have!" [19]And Abraham's faith did not weaken, even though, at about 100 years of age, he figured his body was as good as dead—and so was Sarah's womb.

[20]Abraham never wavered in believing God's promise. In fact, his faith grew stronger, and in this he brought glory to God. [21]He was fully convinced that God is able to do whatever he promises. [22]And because of Abraham's faith, God counted him as righteous. [23]And when God counted him as righteous, it wasn't just for Abraham's benefit. It was recorded [24]for our benefit, too, assuring us that

God will also count us as righteous if we believe in him, the one who raised Jesus our Lord from the dead. [25]He was handed over to die because of our sins, and he was raised to life to make us right with God.

Chapter 5

Therefore, since we have been made right in God's sight by faith, we have peace with God because of what Jesus Christ our Lord has done for us. [2]Because of our faith, Christ has brought us into this place of undeserved privilege where we now stand, and we confidently and joyfully look forward to sharing God's glory.

[3]We can rejoice, too, when we run into problems and trials, for we know that they help us develop endurance. [4]And endurance develops strength of character, and character strengthens our confident hope of salvation. [5]And this hope will not lead to disappointment. For we know how dearly God loves us, because he has given us the Holy Spirit to fill our hearts with his love.

[6]When we were utterly helpless, Christ came at just the right time and died for us sinners. [7]Now, most people would not be willing to die for an upright person, though someone might perhaps be willing to die for a person who is especially good. [8]But God showed his great love for us by sending Christ to die for us while we were still sinners. [9]And since we have been made right in God's sight by the blood of Christ, he will certainly save us from God's condemnation. [10]For since our friendship with God was restored by the death of his Son while we were still his enemies, we will certainly be saved through the life of his Son. [11]So now we can rejoice in our wonderful new relationship with God because our Lord Jesus Christ has made us friends of God.

[12]When Adam sinned, sin entered the world. Adam's sin

brought death, so death spread to everyone, for everyone sinned. [13]Yes, people sinned even before the law was given. But it was not counted as sin because there was not yet any law to break. [14]Still, everyone died—from the time of Adam to the time of Moses—even those who did not disobey an explicit commandment of God, as Adam did. Now Adam is a symbol, a representation of Christ, who was yet to come. [15]But there is a great difference between Adam's sin and God's gracious gift. For the sin of this one man, Adam, brought death to many. But even greater is God's wonderful grace and his gift of forgiveness to many through this other man, Jesus Christ. [16]And the result of God's gracious gift is very different from the result of that one man's sin. For Adam's sin led to condemnation, but God's free gift leads to our being made right with God, even though we are guilty of many sins. [17]For the sin of this one man, Adam, caused death to rule over many. But even greater is God's wonderful grace and his gift of righteousness, for all who receive it will live in triumph over sin and death through this one man, Jesus Christ.

[18]Yes, Adam's one sin brings condemnation for everyone, but Christ's one act of righteousness brings a right relationship with God and new life for everyone. [19]Because one person disobeyed God, many became sinners. But because one other person obeyed God, many will be made righteous.

[20]God's law was given so that all people could see how sinful they were. But as people sinned more and more, God's wonderful grace became more abundant. [21]So just as sin ruled over all people and brought them to death, now God's wonderful grace rules instead, giving us right standing with God and resulting in eternal life through Jesus Christ our Lord.

Chapter 6

Well then, should we keep on sinning so that God can show us more and more of his wonderful grace? [2]Of course not! Since we have died to sin, how can we continue to live in it? [3]Or have you forgotten that when we were joined with Christ Jesus in baptism, we joined him in his death? [4]For we died and were buried with Christ by baptism. And just as Christ was raised from the dead by the glorious power of the Father, now we also may live new lives.

[5]Since we have been united with him in his death, we will also be raised to life as he was. [6]We know that our old sinful selves were crucified with Christ so that sin might lose its power in our lives. We are no longer slaves to sin. [7]For when we died with Christ we were set free from the power of sin. [8]And since we died with Christ, we know we will also live with him. [9]We are sure of this because Christ was raised from the dead, and he will never die again. Death no longer has any power over him. [10]When he died, he died once to break the power of sin. But now that he lives, he lives for the glory of God. [11]So you also should consider yourselves to be dead to the power of sin and alive to God through Christ Jesus.

[12]Do not let sin control the way you live; do not give in to sinful desires. [13]Do not let any part of your body become an instrument of evil to serve sin. Instead, give yourselves completely to God, for you were dead, but now you have new life. So use your whole body as an instrument to do what is right for the glory of God. [14]Sin is no longer your master, for you no longer live under the requirements of the law. Instead, you live under the freedom of God's grace.

[15]Well then, since God's grace has set us free from the law, does that mean we can go on sinning? Of course not!

¹⁶Don't you realize that you become the slave of whatever you choose to obey? You can be a slave to sin, which leads to death, or you can choose to obey God, which leads to righteous living. ¹⁷Thank God! Once you were slaves of sin, but now you wholeheartedly obey this teaching we have given you. ¹⁸Now you are free from your slavery to sin, and you have become slaves to righteous living.

¹⁹Because of the weakness of your human nature, I am using the illustration of slavery to help you understand all this. Previously, you let yourselves be slaves to impurity and lawlessness, which led ever deeper into sin. Now you must give yourselves to be slaves to righteous living so that you will become holy.

²⁰When you were slaves to sin, you were free from the obligation to do right. ²¹And what was the result? You are now ashamed of the things you used to do, things that end in eternal doom. ²²But now you are free from the power of sin and have become slaves of God. Now you do those things that lead to holiness and result in eternal life. ²³For the wages of sin is death, but the free gift of God is eternal life through Christ Jesus our Lord.

Chapter 7

Now, dear brothers and sisters—you who are familiar with the law—don't you know that the law applies only while a person is living? ²For example, when a woman marries, the law binds her to her husband as long as he is alive. But if he dies, the laws of marriage no longer apply to her. ³So while her husband is alive, she would be committing adultery if she married another man. But if her husband dies, she is free from that law and does not commit adultery when she remarries.

⁴So, my dear brothers and sisters, this is the point: You died to the power of the law when you died with Christ.

And now you are united with the one who was raised from the dead. As a result, we can produce a harvest of good deeds for God. [5]When we were controlled by our old nature, sinful desires were at work within us, and the law aroused these evil desires that produced a harvest of sinful deeds, resulting in death. [6]But now we have been released from the law, for we died to it and are no longer captive to its power. Now we can serve God, not in the old way of obeying the letter of the law, but in the new way of living in the Spirit.

[7]Well then, am I suggesting that the law of God is sinful? Of course not! In fact, it was the law that showed me my sin. I would never have known that coveting is wrong if the law had not said, "You must not covet." [8]But sin used this command to arouse all kinds of covetous desires within me! If there were no law, sin would not have that power. [9]At one time I lived without understanding the law. But when I learned the command not to covet, for instance, the power of sin came to life, [10]and I died. So I discovered that the law's commands, which were supposed to bring life, brought spiritual death instead. [11]Sin took advantage of those commands and deceived me; it used the commands to kill me. [12]But still, the law itself is holy, and its commands are holy and right and good.

[13]But how can that be? Did the law, which is good, cause my death? Of course not! Sin used what was good to bring about my condemnation to death. So we can see how terrible sin really is. It uses God's good commands for its own evil purposes.

[14]So the trouble is not with the law, for it is spiritual and good. The trouble is with me, for I am all too human, a slave to sin. [15]I don't really understand myself, for I want to do what is right, but I don't do it. Instead, I do what I hate. [16]But if I know that what I am doing is wrong, this

shows that I agree that the law is good. [17]So I am not the one doing wrong; it is sin living in me that does it.

[18]And I know that nothing good lives in me, that is, in my sinful nature. I want to do what is right, but I can't. [19]I want to do what is good, but I don't. I don't want to do what is wrong, but I do it anyway. [20]But if I do what I don't want to do, I am not really the one doing wrong; it is sin living in me that does it.

[21]I have discovered this principle of life—that when I want to do what is right, I inevitably do what is wrong. [22]I love God's law with all my heart. [23]But there is another power within me that is at war with my mind. This power makes me a slave to the sin that is still within me. [24]Oh, what a miserable person I am! Who will free me from this life that is dominated by sin and death? [25]Thank God! The answer is in Jesus Christ our Lord. So you see how it is: In my mind I really want to obey God's law, but because of my sinful nature I am a slave to sin.

Chapter 8

So now there is no condemnation for those who belong to Christ Jesus. [2]And because you belong to him, the power of the life-giving Spirit has freed you from the power of sin that leads to death. [3]The law of Moses was unable to save us because of the weakness of our sinful nature. So God did what the law could not do. He sent his own Son in a body like the bodies we sinners have. And in that body God declared an end to sin's control over us by giving his Son as a sacrifice for our sins. [4]He did this so that the just requirement of the law would be fully satisfied for us, who no longer follow our sinful nature but instead follow the Spirit.

[5]Those who are dominated by the sinful nature think about sinful things, but those who are controlled by the

Holy Spirit think about things that please the Spirit. [6]So letting your sinful nature control your mind leads to death. But letting the Spirit control your mind leads to life and peace. [7]For the sinful nature is always hostile to God. It never did obey God's laws, and it never will. [8]That's why those who are still under the control of their sinful nature can never please God.

[9]But you are not controlled by your sinful nature. You are controlled by the Spirit if you have the Spirit of God living in you. (And remember that those who do not have the Spirit of Christ living in them do not belong to him at all.) [10]And Christ lives within you, so even though your body will die because of sin, the Spirit gives you life because you have been made right with God. [11]The Spirit of God, who raised Jesus from the dead, lives in you. And just as God raised Christ Jesus from the dead, he will give life to your mortal bodies by this same Spirit living within you.

[12]Therefore, dear brothers and sisters, you have no obligation to do what your sinful nature urges you to do. [13]For if you live by its dictates, you will die. But if through the power of the Spirit you put to death the deeds of your sinful nature, you will live. [14]For all who are led by the Spirit of God are children of God.

[15]So you have not received a spirit that makes you fearful slaves. Instead, you received God's Spirit when he adopted you as his own children. Now we call him, "Abba, Father." [16]For his Spirit joins with our spirit to affirm that we are God's children. [17]And since we are his children, we are his heirs. In fact, together with Christ we are heirs of God's glory. But if we are to share his glory, we must also share his suffering.

[18]Yet what we suffer now is nothing compared to the glory he will reveal to us later. [19]For all creation is waiting

eagerly for that future day when God will reveal who his children really are. [20]Against its will, all creation was subjected to God's curse. But with eager hope, [21]the creation looks forward to the day when it will join God's children in glorious freedom from death and decay. [22]For we know that all creation has been groaning as in the pains of childbirth right up to the present time. [23]And we believers also groan, even though we have the Holy Spirit within us as a foretaste of future glory, for we long for our bodies to be released from sin and suffering. We, too, wait with eager hope for the day when God will give us our full rights as his adopted children, including the new bodies he has promised us. [24]We were given this hope when we were saved. (If we already have something, we don't need to hope for it. [25]But if we look forward to something we don't yet have, we must wait patiently and confidently.)

[26]And the Holy Spirit helps us in our weakness. For example, we don't know what God wants us to pray for. But the Holy Spirit prays for us with groanings that cannot be expressed in words. [27]And the Father who knows all hearts knows what the Spirit is saying, for the Spirit pleads for us believers in harmony with God's own will. [28]And we know that God causes everything to work together for the good of those who love God and are called according to his purpose for them. [29]For God knew his people in advance, and he chose them to become like his Son, so that his Son would be the firstborn among many brothers and sisters. [30]And having chosen them, he called them to come to him. And having called them, he gave them right standing with himself. And having given them right standing, he gave them his glory.

[31]What shall we say about such wonderful things as these? If God is for us, who can ever be against us? [32]Since

he did not spare even his own Son but gave him up for us all, won't he also give us everything else? [33]Who dares accuse us whom God has chosen for his own? No one—for God himself has given us right standing with himself. [34]Who then will condemn us? No one—for Christ Jesus died for us and was raised to life for us, and he is sitting in the place of honor at God's right hand, pleading for us.

[35]Can anything ever separate us from Christ's love? Does it mean he no longer loves us if we have trouble or calamity, or are persecuted, or hungry, or destitute, or in danger, or threatened with death? [36](As the Scriptures say, "For your sake we are killed every day; we are being slaughtered like sheep.") [37]No, despite all these things, overwhelming victory is ours through Christ, who loved us.

[38]And I am convinced that nothing can ever separate us from God's love. Neither death nor life, neither angels nor demons, neither our fears for today nor our worries about tomorrow—not even the powers of hell can separate us from God's love. [39]No power in the sky above or in the earth below—indeed, nothing in all creation will ever be able to separate us from the love of God that is revealed in Christ Jesus our Lord.

The Case for Christ Movie and Story

Watch *The Case for Christ* movie (2017)—a film based on the true story of Lee Strobel's world-famous journalistic investigation into the trustworthiness of Scripture and Jesus Christ's claims. (For added background, check out Strobel's books as well.) Pay close attention to Strobel's authentic search for truth and his desire to have honest and *trustworthy* evidence.

There are several excellent print and online resources to extend your learning with this story and these important topics; do not hesitate to investigate these or go down a rabbit trail exploring this subject matter further.

Jesus says if you seek, you *will* find!

"If you look for me wholeheartedly, you will find me. I will be found by you," says the LORD.
JEREMIAH 29:13-14

THE CASE FOR CHRIST RESPONSES

1. Some key quotes to listen for and respond to (minutes 1–16): "Well, it's not luck. It's Jesus" (6:30). "And I don't believe it was a coincidence that you came to the restaurant. I don't, so . . . what do I do with that?" Write out three questions and a personal journal response to this section of the movie. Share your response with someone you trust, and have a conversation about your questions.

2. Some key quotes to listen for and respond to (minutes 16–41): "Because I'm trying to explain that I felt something that is maybe more real than anything I've ever felt in my whole life!" (18:34). "How could anyone talk about historical evidence for the resurrection?" (22:43). "I understand that a number of people claimed to have seen Jesus after his crucifixion, and some of them even wrote it down, but I guess my question is, how can we be sure of the reliability of those manuscripts?" (37:14). "Why would he do it? Why . . . Why allow himself to be killed, if he really is the Son of God?" (40:24). Write out three questions and a personal journal response to this section of the movie. Share your response with someone you trust, and have a conversation about your questions.

3. Some key quotes to listen for and respond to (minutes 41–109:15): "Do you really want to know the truth, or is your mind made up regardless of the facts?" (47:53). "When is enough evidence enough evidence?" (48:06). "I will give you a new heart. I will put a new

spirit in you. I will remove from you your heart of stone and give you a heart of flesh" (108:42). Write out three questions and a personal journal response to this section of the movie. Share your response with someone you trust, and have a conversation about your questions.

4. Some key quotes to listen for and respond to (minutes 109:15–150): "I missed the truth. I'm sorry—I just didn't see it." "You didn't want to see it'" (134:12). "Believing in God, not believing in God, either way it still takes a leap of faith!" (134:58). "But why would he do it? It's really very simple. Love" (138:58). "Believe" + "Receive" = "Become." (143:20). Write out three questions and a personal journal response to this section of the movie. Share your response with someone you trust, and have a conversation about your questions.

5. Lee Strobel had to admit he was wrong in the shooting case with the story he was writing for the *Chicago Tribune*. He also had to admit he was wrong about God. What might you need to "retract" on your journey to know Christ as the fullness of reality? What does it take for Lee Strobel to admit he was wrong and even publicly say he was wrong?

6. Lee has many conversations with people on his journey throughout the film, some of them often only a few minutes long. What conversations would be helpful for you to have? What trustworthy people could you ask to help you with your questions? Take a bold step and have the first one this week, or even today. Remember 1 Peter 3:15: "But in your hearts revere Christ as Lord. Always be prepared to give an answer to everyone who asks you to give the reason for the hope that you have. But do this with gentleness and respect" (NIV).

7. Jesus says, "Seek, and you will find" (Matthew 7:7). Leslie sought the truth on her own journey through conversations, research, and trust. In a similar yet very different way, Lee committed to finding the truth as well—he invested time, money, energy, and resources to read, travel, and research in order to find the truth. Wherever you are on your journey, what is a good next step for you to grow and strengthen your Christ-centered biblical worldview—to know the Truth?

A Potential Trust List for a Christ-Centered Theist

Big Questions of Life	Christ-Centered Theism ("The Fullness of Christ")
1. What is the nature of reality? What is really real?	Christ-centered theists trust that the spiritual and the material are both real yet independent and interdependent with each other as embodied in the Trinity and made manifest in the person of Jesus, the fullness of the Father, and the oneness of the Holy Spirit. The spiritual realm and material realm are both independently real yet coexist and interact independently, interdependently with, and intra-dependently within each other in various forms, degrees, and ways. The spiritual and material are fully balanced and made perfect in the Trinity.
2. Who or what is God?	Christ-centered theists trust that God is the all-powerful Creator, the sustainer, and the giver of all life. God is perfect and essentially good in nature and being. God is personal. God has full authority. God is the standard for and author of morality. God is triune, three persons—Jesus the Son, God the Father, and God the Holy Spirit—in one God.
3. What is a human being? What is humankind? (Who am I? What am I?)	Christ-centered theists trust that humans are distinct, wonderful creations made in the image of God but not possessing the exact nature of God nor existing as an extension or part of God. Humans possess an individual spirit that is not God's spirit. Jesus is fully man and is the true human who is sinless. Jesus is also fully God. Christ-centered theists trust that the Holy Spirit of God can indwell humans without

Big Questions of Life	Christ-Centered Theism ("The Fullness of Christ")
	each human losing his or her identity as separate from God, yet they can simultaneously find unity with each other and God through the one Holy Spirit of God indwelling each individual. With this unique indwelling of God's Holy Spirit, a human can have eternal life, now and forever, and as complete and perfected in one's true identity as beloved by God.
4. What is the basis of and standard for morality? How do I decide between right and wrong, and who or what is the basis for moral authority?	Christ-centered theists trust that all ethical morality is objective based on the personal, all-powerful nature of God, who is perfect, loving, and good. God's nature and God's Word, past and present, are the standard for morality. Morality is based on the person, words, and actions of Jesus Christ.
5. What happens to humans at death?	Christ-centered theists trust that when humans die, we have received individual perfection and justification through grace and exist eternally in continual relationship with the perfect, personal, loving God, *or* we remain in an imperfect, incomplete state, having rejected salvation through grace, and necessarily exist separated from God. In essence when we die, we actualize our "true self" and exist with God, *or* we are eternally separated from perfection and wholeness.
6. What is the meaning and purpose of human history? What is the essence of human interaction and relationships?	Christ-centered theists trust that history is the true epic adventure story of God's interaction with humankind. Humans are independent, possessing will and identity as selves in communion with others. Jesus' death on the cross and his resurrection are the eucatastrophe and centrality of all of human history.
7. Why are we here? Where are we going? What is the purpose of human existence?	Christ-centered theists trust that at least one reason humans exist is to enjoy and experience a meaningful personal relationship with the Creator and sustainer of life. We exist in order to expand, enjoy, and protect God's Kingdom through the power of God's Holy Spirit. We exist so we can bring joy and honor to God and self—through genuine worship of God, through loving healthy relationships with God and others, and through authentically serving and loving God, self, and others.

The Parable of Grace

For the past fifteen years, I've used an assignment with my classes that has helped them to understand the real differences between idealism and authentic, gospel-centered Christianity. I have the class take a test on the book of Acts, but before giving the students the test, I send an "essential study guide" home with them. Below I've included the study guide. Following this reading, there are questions for reflection and discussion. (You may want to revisit the *Inklings on Philosophy and Worldview* discussion of grace on pages 138–141 and 174–178.)

Dearest philosophy students,

I am so glad that you took the time and effort to read this "study guide." Welcome to another adventure in learning! I do want to remind you that the main goal of my class is to learn; and if you have not noticed yet, learning often comes in a variety of packages. This lesson is packaged in the intricate yet familiar structure of a parable.

We are going to use the traditional evaluation tool of the classic "100-point test" to help learn more about the four different worldviews and salvation through grace. And yes, we will also simultaneously be evaluating your understanding of the book of Acts. We will discuss all of this in more detail in class (and at other times if you wish), but for this part of the lesson, here is the essential information you will need to pass this test.

I know that this test will be nearly impossible for you to pass on your own. Please remember that in class I announced that this is a pass/fail test. To pass, you need a perfect score. Without a perfect score, you fail, which for this test equals a *zero*. I want to clarify that I am intentionally designing a few of the questions on this test so that the apostle Paul himself might have a hard time getting a perfect score. For example, since the evaluation is about the book of Acts, I can ask *anything* from the book on the test. Basically, unless you have memorized the text in the next two weeks, you would not be able to answer this type of question: "What is the fifth word on the tenth line on such and such page?" or "What is the exact wording of such and such verse in the tenth chapter"? Notice how this type of evaluation fits with an idealist's or even a religious Christian theist's philosophy, which demands absolute perfection.

The *one way* you can ensure that you will pass this test is to trust your teacher to provide another way. Your teacher has taken the test and achieved a perfect score and is willing to give you his grade as a free gift. You will receive a perfect score on this test *by asking for one* and believing that you will receive one. Please note: your performance on the test, which you will still take, has no effect on your score of 100 percent—unless, of course, you choose to not have a 100-percent grade going into the test and try to achieve this perfect score through your own diligence and hard work. Be aware that the choice is yours: you have a zero on the test right now; you may choose to ask for and receive a perfect score *before* you take the test, or you may choose to accept your current zero for now and strive for a perfect score on your own through taking the test and accepting the score you get. Remember: you could simply believe that I will do what I say, and you can ask for a perfect grade and thus receive your perfect score in advance as a free gift.

Please note: this perfect score will be irrevocably granted to all who believe that I will do this and ask me to do it *before* the test is taken. You will receive the perfect score in my grade book as soon as you believe and ask. Nothing you do or say will take that grade out of my grade book unless you ask me to do so in person with two or more witnesses and in writing. As you prepare for your test, enjoy the freedom and peace that comes with real grace.

I hope to see or hear from you soon. I love having you in class; it is a joy and honor to learn and grow with you. Embrace the grace.

With joy and love,
Mr. Dominguez

PS I hope and trust that this is "good news" for you. You *are* encouraged to share this news with your fellow classmates.

The Parable of Grace: Reflection and Discussion

Consider the following quotes about grace from the Bible, and use the questions for personal reflection and discussion.

God saved you by his grace when you believed. And you can't take credit for this; it is a gift from God. Salvation is not a reward for the good things we have done, so none of us can boast about it.

EPHESIANS 2:8-9

If you openly declare that Jesus is Lord and believe in your heart that God raised him from the dead, you will be saved. For it is by believing in your heart that you are made right with God, and it is by openly declaring your faith that you are saved.

ROMANS 10:9-10

This is how God loved the world: He gave his one and only Son, so that everyone who believes in him will not perish but have eternal life.

JOHN 3:16

1. What do these verses reveal about God's grace to us? How is this grace modeled in the parable of grace?

2. Compare and contrast idealism and authentic, gospel-centered Christianity as seen in the parable of grace.

3. Why has God chosen to save humanity by grace?

4. What does being saved by grace do for a person's motivation to serve and love God?

5. What are the limits to this metaphor? Where does it break down?

The Truman Show and You

Find and watch the movie *The Truman Show* (or at least the last thirty minutes) with part 3 of the *Inklings on Philosophy and Worldview* book in mind. Pay close attention to the "Allegory of the Cave" allusions. Then answer these questions.

1. Christof says, "We accept the reality with which we are presented." How does this idea connect with the chandelier and "silly strips" metaphors (see pages 121–130 in the book)?

2. Truman suspects that some of the reality he is living is wrong. (Be sure to note, and ponder, the allegory of the cave metaphor for this entire film.) What does he do to find the truth? What are you currently doing to find the truth?

3. What is Truman willing to risk to find the truth—to get real love? What does real love entail? What are you willing to risk?

4. Truman encounters real love in a character who calls herself Lauren (her real name is Sylvia), and that encounter leads him on a quest for a relationship with the one who has given him this real love. Real love is his core motivation. His recreated patchwork picture of Sylvia is his guide and map and hope for finding the real person beyond the picture and beyond the walls of the fabricated world. How does this relate to our journey toward Christ?

> *"For I know the plans I have for you," says the LORD. "They are plans for good and not for disaster, to give you a future and a hope. In those days when you pray, I will listen. **If you look for me wholeheartedly, you will find me.** I will be found by you," says the LORD. "I will end your captivity and restore your fortunes. I will gather you out of the nations where I sent you and will bring you home again to your own land."*
> JEREMIAH 29:11-14

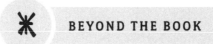

"This Is Not a Pipe"

After reading chapter 21 in the *Inklings* book, find a copy online (or elsewhere) of "The Treachery of Images" by painter René Magritte. The text on the image translates to "This is not a pipe." Consider the following quotes and how they reflect on Magritte's "The Treachery of Images," and then complete the learning adventure on pages 322–323.

We are told that Christ was killed for us, that His death has washed out our sins, and that by dying He disabled death itself. That is the formula. That is Christianity. That is what has to be believed. Any theories we build up as to how Christ's death did all this are, in my view, quite secondary: mere plans or diagrams to be left alone if they do not help us, and, even if they do help us, not to be confused with the thing itself.

C. S. LEWIS, *MERE CHRISTIANITY*

A map *is not* the territory it represents, but, if correct, it has a *similar structure* to the territory, which accounts for its usefulness.

ALFRED KORZYBSKI, *SCIENCE AND SANITY*

To them God has chosen to make known among the Gentiles
the glorious riches of this mystery, which is Christ in you,
the hope of glory.
COLOSSIANS 1:27, NIV

Jesus told [Thomas], "I am the way, the truth, and the life.
No one can come to the Father except through me."
JOHN 14:6

[Draw or paste a copy of your own version of Magritte's painting below.]

"This Is Not a Pipe": Reflection and Discussion

Write or discuss your answers to the questions below.

1. Where have you possibly replaced the image of the truth for the living person of the Truth?

2. Describe a scenario where you have known *about* a person—a movie star, celebrity, famous person from history, or person on social media—but not actually known the person as a friend or even met the person in real life. What are some of the differences between knowing about someone and having a real, meaningful relationship with someone?

3. What do you need to do to possibly deepen or start a real relationship with Christ? If you do not know the answer to this question, who has taken this step that you could talk with about this journey of relationship?

EXTEND YOUR LEARNING: Take some time (at least twenty minutes) to reflectively and prayerfully contemplate the depth of this vital lesson on the reality of the person of Christ. (I recommend a quiet favorite spot, a beautiful patch of creation, or a walk in a nature preserve.) Ask God to show you the life-giving truths in this lesson that you need right now and for the next stage of your journey. Ask God to reveal himself to you in a personal and powerful way that you will trust as authentic. Respond to this experience in writing or by recording an audio journal. After this, write down your answer to this question: What next steps could you take to grow in your personal connection with God? Consider making this a daily exercise.

The Encounter

Pilate asks, "What is truth?" in John 18:38. Yet the Truth is standing right in front of him. The Roman quest for truth was for an abstract concept, or a set of ideas, or the right string of words.

However, the Truth is a being, *the* being—the living God. John says the Word, the "Logos," became flesh (see John 1:14). The Truth is incarnational, "in the flesh." The Truth is the person right in front of Pilate. In John 14:6, Jesus says, "I am the way, the truth, and the life." In John 20:16-18, Mary has a powerful encounter with Jesus. She actually gets the first hug from the risen Savior. She literally hugs the Truth—and then becomes the first evangelist!

This is the concept of "perichoresis" embodied in Jesus. The Trinity is perpetually inviting all of us, the beloved, into the divine dance of his love.

Look up a definition of *perichoresis* before answering the questions below. The following quote is an example of one definition of perichoresis:

The theologians in the early church tried to describe this wonderful reality that we call Trinity. If any of you have ever been to a Greek wedding, you may have seen their distinctive way of dancing. . . . It's called perichoresis. There are not two dancers, but at least three. They start to go in circles, weaving in and out in this very beautiful pattern of motion. They start to go faster and faster and faster, all the while staying in perfect rhythm and in sync with each other. Eventually, they are dancing so quickly (yet so effortlessly) that as you look at them, it just becomes a blur. Their individual identities are part of a larger dance. The early church fathers and mothers looked at that dance (perichoresis) and said, "That's what the Trinity is like." It's a harmonious set of relationship in which there is mutual giving and receiving. This relationship is called love, and it's what the Trinity is all about. The perichoresis is the dance of love.

JONATHAN MARLOWE

Write down the definition you found (and where you found it) here:

I am praying not only for these disciples but also for all who will ever believe in me through their message. I pray that they will all be one, just as you and I are one—as you are in me, Father, and I am in you. And may they be in us so that the world will believe you sent me. "I have given them the glory you gave me, so they may be one as we are one."

JOHN 17:20-22

1. What does it mean to have an authentic encounter and relationship with the living, loving God of the universe?

2. How does this connect with the definition of *perichoresis*?

3. Describe the unique personal touch in the following encounters Jesus has with people in the Bible. How does the concept of perichoresis fit these passages?

   + A conversation with the woman at the well in John 4:

   + Dignity for the woman caught in adultery in John 8:1-11:

   + A conversation with Nicodemus in John 3:1-21:

   + Dinner with Zacchaeus in Luke 19:1-10:

+ Peter walking on the water in Matthew 14:22-33:

+ Thomas and Jesus in John 20:24-29:

+ The two disciples' walk to Emmaus with Jesus in Luke 24:13-34:

+ The coming of the Holy Spirit at Pentecost in Acts 2:

+ Paul's divine encounter on the road to Damascus in Acts 9:1-19:

The Aslan Moment

Read or reacquaint yourself with one or more books in C. S. Lewis's Chronicles of Narnia series. List and describe as many "Aslan moments" as you can—those times when Aslan appears on the scene. For example, see Edmund's encounter with Aslan after Edmund's time with the White Witch (from *The Lion, the Witch and the Wardrobe*); Lucy's ability to see Aslan when the others cannot see him (from *Prince Caspian*); Eustace's encounter with Aslan when Eustace is a dragon (from *The Voyage of the Dawn Treader*); Shasta's encounter near the end of his journey (from *The Horse and His Boy*); and Emeth's encounter at the end of *The Last Battle*. Note the transformative power of each encounter on the characters.

+ "Aslan moment":

+ "Aslan moment":

+ "Aslan moment":

+ "Aslan moment":

+ "Aslan moment":

+ "Aslan moment":

+ "Aslan moment":

Thoughts and questions to ponder, journal about, or discuss:

1. How is one moment different from another?

2. What does each moment say about each of the characters in those stories being on an *individual* journey? And what does each encounter say about Aslan's timing for each individual character?

3. Aslan says to Shasta in *The Horse and His Boy*, "Child . . . I am telling you your story, not hers. I tell no one any story but his own."* How does this statement reflect our need for a grace-filled and trusting understanding of God and his timing for our individual encounters on each of our journeys?

---

* C. S. Lewis, *The Horse and His Boy* (New York: HarperCollins, 2002), 176.

The Invitation to Love

Read the following poem and then discuss or write down your answers to the questions:

AS KINGFISHERS CATCH FIRE

As kingfishers catch fire, dragonflies draw flame;
As tumbled over rim in roundy wells
Stones ring; like each tucked string tells, each hung bell's
Bow swung finds tongue to fling out broad its name;
Each mortal thing does one thing and the same:
Deals out that being indoors each one dwells;
Selves—goes itself; myself it speaks and spells,
Crying What I do is me: for that I came.

I say more: the just man justices;
Keeps grace: that keeps all his goings graces;
Acts in God's eye what in God's eye he is —
Christ—for Christ plays in ten thousand places,
Lovely in limbs, and lovely in eyes not his
To the Father through the features of men's faces.

GERARD MANLEY HOPKINS

1. How can the last few lines connect us with the focus of part 3: Christ as the fullness of reality?

2. How can this poem help us connect with Christ and not just with a philosophy or a concept about Christ?

3. How can this poem help us live out the inspiring biblical truths presented to us in 1 Corinthians 12? (See also the "Celebrations of Gifts" project on pages 337–338 of this guidebook.)

The Power of Love

One of the main goals of this guidebook is to guide you into practical application of the information in this book and the *Inklings* book, which now culminates with an invitation to a lifestyle and worldview of love. Paul admonishes the saints in Corinth about this in his letter to them. He states, "Knowledge puffs up, while love builds up" (1 Corinthians 8:1, NIV). Consider this passage from 1 John about love:

> Dear friends, let us continue to love one another, for love comes from God. Anyone who loves is a child of God and knows God. But anyone who does not love does not know God, for God is love.
>
> God showed how much he loved us by sending his one and only Son into the world so that we might have eternal life through him. This is real love—not that we loved God, but that he loved us and sent his Son as a sacrifice to take away our sins.
>
> Dear friends, since God loved us that much, we surely ought to love each other. No one has ever seen God. But if we love each other, God lives in us, and his love is brought to full expression in us.

And God has given us his Spirit as proof that we live in him and he in us. Furthermore, we have seen with our own eyes and now testify that the Father sent his Son to be the Savior of the world. All who declare that Jesus is the Son of God have God living in them, and they live in God. We know how much God loves us, and we have put our trust in his love.

God is love, and all who live in love live in God, and God lives in them. And as we live in God, our love grows more perfect. So we will not be afraid on the day of judgment, but we can face him with confidence because we live like Jesus here in this world.

Such love has no fear, because perfect love expels all fear. If we are afraid, it is for fear of punishment, and this shows that we have not fully experienced his perfect love. We love each other because he loved us first.

1 JOHN 4:7-19

In light of the verses above and the entire focus of part 3, have a candid conversation with someone you trust about your answers to the following questions. Consider not only dialoguing but also praying with a mentor, teacher, pastor, coach, parent, relative, or good friend who understands the concepts in these texts. A reading of 1 Corinthians 13 (see page 121) will be a helpful reminder of the definition of biblical love.

1. How is the desire to be authentically loved by God and the call to truly love God and others the ultimate motivator and goal for us on our worldview quest?

2. Do you love God? Do you love *God*, not just the idea or concept
   or stories about God? If so, what could you do to grow in your love
   for God? What does authentic, loving intimacy with God look like
   for you? If you do not have this type of relationship with the living,
   loving God of the universe, how will you recognize it when you
   find it, how will you pursue it, and how will you maintain it?

3. Ask God what is keeping you from loving God, or loving God
   more. Love and trust go hand in hand. Do you trust God? If not,
   why not? What needs to happen for you to be able to put God on
   your trust list?

4. Do you love yourself? Do you like yourself? God not only loves
   you; he adores you; he delights in you; he calls you his beloved!
   (See Zephaniah 3:17.) What would it take for you to see yourself as
   God sees you, to love yourself as God loves you? In John 3:16 Jesus
   says, "God so loved the world." This includes *you*. Paul reminds us
   in Romans 5 that God loves us even while we are sinners, so don't
   use that as an excuse. How can you grow in loving yourself as God
   loves you? (Keep in mind that people often confuse self-love with

selfishness; selfishness comes when you love only yourself, at the expense of loving others.)

5. Are you loving others? What does it look like for us to love others as God loves others? Consider your recent reading of John—how does Jesus show us how to truly love others? What is implied in the statement "Love your neighbor as you love yourself"? Jesus even encourages us to love our enemies. How can you grow in loving all people?

6. What are practical ways that the philosophical approach to worldview in the *Inklings* book and guidebook invites all of us into building relationships of love and honor for everyone regardless of what they believe?

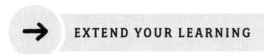

Part Three Projects

CELEBRATION OF GIFTS CREATIVE PROJECT

God has given each of you a gift from his great variety of
spiritual gifts. Use them well to serve one another.
1 PETER 4:10

In his grace, God has given us different gifts for doing certain
things well.
ROMANS 12:6

There are different kinds of spiritual gifts, but the same Spirit is
the source of them all. There are different kinds of service, but
we serve the same Lord. God works in different ways, but it is
the same God who does the work in all of us.
1 CORINTHIANS 12:4

These verses are the primary foundation for this activity. Connecting
philosophy and worldview with your unique giftedness is a great way
to concretize some of the abstract lessons we have encountered in these

texts. Have fun making a creative project. A primary objective for this type of project is to utilize your giftedness to create something original and unique that has to do with your journey through part 3. Find a way to do what you love and weave it into what you have learned on this philosophy adventure. Write a poem, take some photos, write a story, make some T-shirts, connect with athletics, make a poster, research some songs, write a song—the project is open-ended and limited only by your creativity.

DIGGING DEEPER WITH THE CHANDELIER METAPHOR

This project encourages you to go deeper with the chandelier learning adventures on pages 231–255. The guidebook offers some examples of "lights on," "lights off," and "Christ." With regard to this metaphor, I stated, "Remember, these examples are simply meant to get you started. Use these first steps to go deeper into your understanding." You have the rest of your life to discover more and more of these truths about where we do and do not see Christ in the four worldviews, but why not get started right now? Where can you add to each of these categories for the four worldviews? All truth comes from God—where do you see truth (light) in each of these worldviews that points us to Christ? Using the truths of "general revelation" and "special revelation," what are more aspects of Christ found in each of the answers to the seven questions for the four worldviews?

EXTEND YOUR LEARNING: Think back through this entire course of study. What has stuck out to you the most? What are you still pondering? What was your favorite lesson? Where was your most profound epiphany? Take one or two of these ideas and extend your learning by reading another book on that topic, go on another learning adventure, do some extended research, or engage in some more life-giving conversations. Go on a field trip to visit a museum or place of worship that is new for you. Start a worldview journal. This activity is not only a great way to punctuate the close of this text but is also an effective way to continue your learning adventures.

FURTHER READING
FOR THE JOURNEY

This guidebook has been designed to help you continue your journey of discovery of the Truth himself.

Many authors have helped me get to where I am on my journey. Listed below are some suggestions as next steps to encourage you as you continue the adventure.

Be sure to check out additional resources, videos, podcasts, and learning adventures at InTheTrueMyth.org.

PHILOSOPHY AND WORLDVIEW

The Abolition of Man, C. S. Lewis
Miracles, C. S. Lewis
The Problem of Pain, C. S. Lewis
The Universe Next Door, James Sire
The Everlasting Man, G. K. Chesterton
Who Is This Man?, John Ortberg
The Art of Letting Go, Richard Rohr
Eager to Love, Richard Rohr
New Seeds of Contemplation, Thomas Merton
On the Incarnation, Athanasius

JOURNEY AND QUEST

Love Does, Bob Goff
Culture of Honor, Danny Silk
If You Want to Walk on Water, You've Got to Get Out of the Boat,
    John Ortberg
Keep Your Love On, Danny Silk
The Return of the Prodigal Son, Henri Nouwen
The Horse and His Boy, C. S. Lewis
The Great Divorce, C. S. Lewis
The Screwtape Letters, C. S. Lewis
*Bandersnatch: C. S. Lewis, J. R. R. Tolkien, and the Creative
    Collaboration of the Inklings*, Dianna Paulac Glyes
The Life of the Beloved, Henri Nouwen

Trust in the LORD with all your heart; do not depend on your
own understanding.
PROVERBS 3:5